MAKI SALE HAPPEN BEFORE LUNCH

50 CUT-TO-THE-CHASE STRATEGIES FOR GETTING THE BUSINESS RESULTS YOU WANT

STEPHAN SCHIFFMAN

New York   Chicago   San Francisco   Lisbon   London   Madrid   Mexico City
Milan   New Delhi   San Juan   Seoul   Singapore   Sydney   Toronto

1 2 3 4 5 6 7 8 9 0   QFR/QFR   1 6 5 4 3 2 1

ISBN   978-0-07-178868-7
MHID   0-07-178868-9

e-ISBN   978-0-07-178869-4
e-MHID   0-07-178869-7

This publication is designed to provide accurate and authoritative information in regard to the subject matter covered. It is sold with the understanding
that the author nor the publisher is not engaged in rendering legal, accounting, or other professional service. If legal advice or other expert assistance is
required, the services of a competent professional person should be sought.
            —*From a Declaration of Principles jointly*
                adopted by a Committee of the American Bar
                Association and a Committee of Publishers.

McGraw-Hill books are available at special quantity discounts to use as
premiums and sales promotions, or for use in corporate training programs.
To contact a representative please e-mail us at bulksales@mcgraw-hill.com.

This book is printed on acid-free paper.

In memory of Jean Zanger

Contents

PART TWO
MAKE SOMETHING HAPPEN BY. . . USING A
PROCESS THAT GETS YOU TO THE NEXT STEP

PART THREE
MAKE SOMETHING HAPPEN BY . . .
TOUGHING IT OUT UNTIL YOU CATCH A BREAK

Introduction

Back in 1980, I first read a book about the famous literary agent Irving "Swifty" Lazar. At that time, he was one of the most important people in all of Hollywood, and each year he threw fabulous parties, crowded with famous and wildly successful people whom he represented.

He was fortunate in his own right, of course. The reason, which became clear in the book, was that he understood the need to make things happen for him, and his philosophy has stayed with me ever since.

Some years later, I was talking to the owner of a major New York company. In the course of our sales conversation, I asked him how he had happened to start his business nearly 40 years previously. He had had a $35 truck (Yes, you read that correctly: a $35 truck!), and he went door to door selling security systems. Each evening, he counted the number of people that he had spoken to during the day, the number of companies that had signed on, and the number that had said no to him.

He told me that when he made a sale, it took about five weeks from the time he did the system installation to the time he got paid. Of course, while he was doing the installation, he wasn't driving the truck and talking to people.

Hold that thought for a moment, and consider the following as well: when I first started selling my sales training courses, I made a series of cold calls every day. My goal was to actually speak to someone, meet with him, sell sales training, conduct the program, and then—and only then—get paid. From the moment that I started with the cold call until the day I received payment averaged three months. That's 90 days.

Now let's take these stories and combine them into the lesson that I want you to take from this book and translate into your world.

First, consider Swifty Lazar. He realized that if he did not do something each day, then nothing would happen to help him achieve his success. Every day *before lunch*, Swifty made a point of finding something that would benefit him or his company. He knew that it was easy to stay busy doing "stuff" and accomplish nothing.

Next, think about the guy with the $35 truck. He knew that there would be times when he wasn't contacting new customers because he was performing installations. But he also knew that this meant that on the days when he wasn't installing security systems, he'd better be out driving around and talking to prospects. The minute he stopped, his business would dry up.

Finally, I add my own example. The three-month lag time between the first cold call and payment for my services meant that I had to constantly keep those cold calls going, lining up new business. I couldn't afford to rest on my laurels and congratulate myself on what a great salesperson I was. Still less could I afford to be constantly distracted by small issues that pulled me away from cold calls.

As a salesperson, you know that it is easy to become consumed by customer issues, small talk, coffee, or, for that matter, *anything* but selling. The solution: self-discipline and keeping your eye on the big goal.

First, every day, make an appointment with yourself. Decide what is the single most important item in your sales day and focus on that.

Second, make sure that you understand your sales cycle. Most people never think about it. However, if you want to make money in 90 days, and your sales cycle is 90 days long, you had better do something today, not tomorrow.

Several months ago, I was working with a sales force. The reps had all had a great quarter. They were ecstatic with their commissions, which was understandable. But they were making a crucial mistake: they believed that they could afford to sit back and take some mental time off—which quickly translated into taking some real time off. They stopped working.

They did not realize that their results in the next 90 days depended on what they did today. Their success in the previous quarter was the end result of the work they had done in the past 90 days, or up to three months ago.

In July I walked into a training meeting and said to a sales force of 20 people, "How was your September?" There was confused silence for a few minutes, and then someone said, "Do you mean last year?"

"No," I replied, "I mean this September. Because the work that you've done this past month is going to bear fruit in September. From your point of view, September is already over! Get it?" (After some further discussion, they got it.)

I start every day by thinking what I can do that will better my life and my sales experience. My mind is focused on the future, and since, as I told you, it takes me 90 days from the time I call someone until I get paid, I am always looking 90 days ahead . . . every day . . . every day . . . every day. The minute I stop is the minute my business starts to fall apart.

So what is the lesson? You can make a sale each day before lunch if you *start* each day before lunch. In sales, it is about the starts, not the end. *Start something every day.*

Always set an appointment with yourself to prospect.

Realize and know your sales cycle.

Start every day with a new attitude.

Follow those three rules, and in your life and your career, you'll make things happen.

—STEPHAN SCHIFFMAN
September 2011

PART ONE

Make Something Happen by . . . Getting Obsessed About the Right Stuff

1   Throw out the Ball

The legendary agent Irving "Swifty" Lazar had a motto: "Make something happen before lunch."

Many people think that, in holding to this motto, Lazar meant that his goal was to finalize a new deal every day before lunch. Something tells me, though, that even with a client list that included such luminaries as Humphrey Bogart, Vladimir Nabokov, Truman Capote, Richard Nixon, Jeanne Kirkpatrick, and many, many others, Lazar probably didn't close a movie deal or land a multimillion-dollar book contract every single business day of the year. After all, there are at least 250 working days in a year. That's a lot of books and movies to sell! So what did Lazar mean when he talked about "making something happen"?

Here's one theory. Perhaps Hollywood's greatest agent simply meant that he wanted to move at least one relationship *forward* each and every day. In fact, I believe that that daily habit — identifying something two people can agree is worth moving forward on — is a recipe for success in virtually every area of human endeavor.

Let me give you an example of what I mean. You're about to read dialogues from two telephone calls that actually took place. Each call moved its relationship forward to a new stage. People who follow Lazar's example, and make things happen before lunch, get into the habit of asking for action in this way — and measuring the relationship by what happens next.

> *When you ask openly for action, you find out whether your relationship is "alive."*

The first exchange was a call I made to the CEO of a major national telecommunications company. Initially, he was resistant to meet with me. Before I'd made contact with him on that call, he'd never heard of me or my organization. Here's how the call concluded:

> Me: I'd really like to meet with you to so we can talk about what we've been able to do for some of the companies in your industry.
>
> Prospect: (Cutting in.) Why don't you just send me some literature first so I can get a better idea of what your company does?
>
> Me: Actually, I really prefer not to mail literature. Why don't we just get together instead? How's next Wednesday at one?
>
> (Pause.)
>
> Prospect: Ahh. Gee, Wednesday's booked. It would have to be Friday.
>
> Me: Friday, then. One o'clock?
>
> Prospect: Okay. Friday at one.

By standing my ground and making a concrete suggestion for a date and time, I was able to set an appointment. That face-to-face meeting eventually turned into a sales training contract, one that was worth well over a quarter of a million dollars. It was a good thing I asked for the meeting that second time!

How about the other exchange? Well, this was a call that allowed me to move forward on my goal of re-recruiting a superb trainer named Steve Bookbinder. Steve had once worked for us, but had decided to change course and to seek opportunities elsewhere. Meanwhile, our training business grew, and grew, and grew. Before long, we had reached a point where we needed someone who knew our company's material inside and out, who could handle a new program on a moment's notice, and who could deliver our training sessions with unparalleled authority and confidence. Since we pride ourselves on hiring trainers who really do sell on the front lines, the person also had to be an extraordinary sales professional. That was a tall order!

The call I made started the process that brought Steve back to our company. I remember it clearly. Here's how it wrapped up:

> Me: You know what? I think you should come in and talk to me about working for us again.
> (Pause.)
> Steve: Well, how do I know it's the right step?
> Me: Let's talk about it. Come in to the office. We'll go over everything. Come in on Monday morning. Let's find a way to make sure this step matches up with what you want to do next.
> Steve: Look, I'm flattered. It's just — I don't want to make a mistake.
> Me: We're not going to make a mistake. Why don't you come in so we can talk it over?
> Steve: You're sure?
> Me: I'm sure. It's time to come home.
> Steve: All right. We'll talk it over. I'll see you Monday.

Since Steve rejoined our company, he's become our lead trainer and once again claimed his place as an invaluable member of the sales team. Steve has had a lot to do with the dramatic growth we've experienced in the past six years. But that's not why I'm telling you about the call.

What I want you to notice is that, in each of the two calls, I *did not attain my objective instantly.* I had to resume control of the conversation (tactfully, but firmly) and reposition myself to set up action that would allow me to discuss something that I firmly believed to be in the interests of both parties.

I had to stay focused, had to keep from getting flustered, and had to avoid getting sidetracked. Most important of all, I had to *suggest a specific course of action* without apology or hesitation.

I had to take responsibility for making something happen — for moving the relationship forward.

During our sales training programs, we always toss out a small plastic ball toward one of the participants. Ninety-nine times out of a hundred, the person we throw the ball to catches it and throws it back. Why do you suppose we would build something like that into a training program for salespeople?

Building relationships with business contacts is a lot like playing ball. We have to take responsibility for getting prospects to play ball with us. We have to take the initiative to throw the ball out in the first place. When we do this, the other person must react somehow — by dropping the ball, or by deflecting it, or by avoiding it altogether, or by catching it and throwing it back. Often, we have to be ready to throw the ball again, so the other person can catch it.

But we do have to take the initiative to throw the ball first. We have to say, "Let's meet Wednesday so I can tell you about what we've been able to do for other companies in your industry." We have to say, "Come in on Monday morning so we can talk about how to make this work for you the second time around."

To get the most we possibly can out of our lives and our relationships, we have to take responsibility for making something happen. We have to ask for action from the other person. I believe this principle applies to everyone, not just to salespeople. Not all of us earn a living as professional salespeople, but we are all selling ideas to everyone we meet all the time. And that means we all stand to benefit by learning how to move relationships forward.

This book is about selling your ideas, whether that means getting an appointment from a reluctant CEO, winning the allegiance of a potential superstar contributor, or accomplishing virtually anything else that's worthwhile and involves other people.

I sell each and every day — and so do you, whether you realize it or not. In fact, everyone sells. But not everyone sells effectively. To sell effectively, you have to be willing to practice asking for action, not just once, but several times. Tactfully, of course. But you do have to ask. That's the secret of making something happen before lunch. Ultimately, that's what all 50 of the rules in this book are about.

The most successful people I know are those who have made a habit of taking the initiative in their business relationships. They persistently "throw out the ball" — just as I did in the two conversations you read a moment ago — to see what happens. The art of making something happen before lunch is nothing more or less than the art of throwing out enough balls, and getting the right people to play ball with you.

Think about that for a moment. If I throw a ball to you, and you catch it and throw it back to me, there's a relationship. By the same token, if you catch the ball, drop it on the floor, and turn and walk away, there really *isn't* a relationship yet. But at least I know where I stand!

In this book, you will learn how to get the right people to play ball with you. You will learn how to take the initiative, throw out a suggestion, and move your relationship forward to a Next Step that makes sense to both parties. With practice, that habit of throwing out the ball will become second nature to you. And you'll be on your way to mastering the neglected art of making something happen before lunch.

MAKE IT HAPPEN PRINCIPLE 1

Successful people find a way to move their relationships forward by "throwing out the ball" — directly suggesting a specific course of action.

RULE 2
Obsession Without Discipline Equals Chaos

If you'd been driving through California's dusty Sacramento Valley in the late 1940s, you might have seen a small boy gathering walnuts in a deserted field.

As your Packard or Studebaker whizzed past, you might have noticed that the boy was gathering English walnuts, not the more common black walnuts. And if you'd have pulled over to ask why he was doing that, the boy would have been able to give you a reason: English walnuts could fetch $5 per 100-pound sack, while black walnuts brought just $3 per 100-pound sack.

He knew why he did what he did.

If you'd driven through Santa Barbara a few months later, you might well have seen the same boy selling eggs door to door. If you'd asked him why he'd gotten out of walnuts, he would have been able to give you a reason. The return from selling eggs door to door was measurably greater than the return he'd been getting from selling walnuts.

He knew why he did what he did.

And if you'd driven through Santa Barbara a couple of years after that, you just might have caught a glimpse of the same young fellow on the local golf course. If you'd asked him why he'd stopped selling the eggs and started working as a caddy, he would have had a reason for you. Caddying offered an even better return than gathering walnuts or selling eggs door to door.

He knew why he did what he did.

In fact, if you'd been able to follow each and every key point of that young man's career from that moment on, you would have seen the same evidence of careful analysis in every new endeavor. If you'd somehow been able to crawl inside that young man's mind as he planned his hour, his day, his month, my bet is that you would have heard this fellow ask himself a few simple questions over and over and over again.

- What's the likely return on this activity?
- Is this activity bringing me closer to my goals?
- What else could I be doing with my time?

The boy's name was Charles Schwab. In later years, he would become a pioneer in the discount brokerage business, and be named to *Money* magazine's elite list of seven people exerting the greatest influence on the American economy. In recent years, Schwab's brokerage firm was estimated at $300 billion.

This habit of having a reason for doing something — preferably a *measurable* reason — was one that served Schwab well in his younger days, and continues to serve him well today. It can serve you well right now. If you know what you're planning to do next with a business contact, but don't know why you're planning to do it, step back and take another look at your daily and weekly schedule. Ask yourself the three questions you just read. Then take out your personal planner and reschedule your day.

Knowing *why* you are undertaking any given task with someone else means knowing what the payoff or return within a given period is likely to be. People who make things happen understand that there must be a reason — a justification — for everything to which they devote a significant chunk of time. (I define "significant chunks of time" as those occupying 15 minutes or more of my day.) You have to track these things, because failing to do so means there is a lack of discipline in your daily routine. If you have no discipline, all the commitment, all the motivation, all the obsession in the world won't propel you toward your goals. Don't misunderstand. Obsession is important, because without it you won't have the energy and focus you need to make things happen. But obsession without order equals chaos.

When I was just getting started with my business, I made it my mission to track everything I did. I had to evaluate whether any given activity was moving me closer to, or further away from, the goals I had set for myself. I kept a log book and made an entry for every quarter hour I spent over the course of the day. I saved all my logs and evaluated them at the end of the week. Next to each entry I placed a plus sign, a zero, or a minus sign. A plus sign meant I was certain that the activity had moved me closer to a key goal. A zero meant I had not moved any closer to one of my goals as a result of the activity, but had not lost any ground either. (I also used zero to identify activities that I wasn't sure about.) Minus signs went next to activities that I was certain had moved me further away from my goals.

10

As I planned the week to come, I always found ways to build my days around activities I knew had a measurable likelihood of moving me closer to what I wanted to accomplish. When I reached out to other people, I made sure I was trying to win a commitment to action on something that moved me forward to a key goal.

For years I've been telling the people who take our programs that *obsession without discipline equals chaos*. I can't tell you how many times I've met with people who have great passion for what they hope to do in life . . . but no idea whether the activities they've placed in their daily schedule are supporting that passion. It's good to have an obsession, but it's not enough!

> *Yes, you must be obsessed with your goals...*
> *but without discipline you will get nowhere!*

For more on setting intelligent goals, see Rule 21. For in-depth advice on time management, see Rule 38.

Before you move on to those parts of the book, though, remember that monitoring your own activity and identifying those tasks that bring you closer to your goals are mandatory steps for making good things happen on a regular basis.

Passion and discipline are two sides of the same principle. That which you are obsessive and passionate about should be important enough for you to measure and reevaluate on a regular basis. That which you measure should inspire enough excitement and energy to motivate you each and every day.

If you cannot follow the young Charles Schwab's example and explain exactly *why* you have stopped doing one thing and started doing another, stop and reevaluate what

11

you're doing. Until you do, all the passion and excitement in the world won't point you toward the activities that move your most important business relationships forward.

MAKE IT HAPPEN PRINCIPLE 2

*Passion is an important prerequisite for success,
but it doesn't work on its own.*

RULE 3 — Act Where You Want to Be, Not Where You Are

"Where are we going, boys?"
"To the top, Johnny!"
"To the top of what, boys?"
"To the Toppermost of the Poppermost, Johnny!"

That's a specially constructed, mind-clearing ritual dialogue that a young rhythm guitarist by the name of John Lennon forced on his scruffy bandmates long before the advent of Beatlemania. Why do you imagine he made the group play such a game?

Picture the four of them trying to motivate themselves to play another all-night set of rock 'n' roll standards — for which they would receive starvation wages. Picture Lennon staring out at a nearly deserted dance floor. Picture four ill-fed young men getting ready to take the stage in a rough-and-tumble tavern in front of yet another tiny and hostile audience.

Lennon was the band's undisputed leader during its difficult and tumultuous early years. He used his odd little "where are we going" ritual often to transform the emotional environment by asking himself — and his colleagues — a simple question: "Where are we going, boys?"

Where are *you* going?

People who make things happen don't get sidetracked by the challenges of the present. They constantly remind themselves of where they're going. They pull the future into the present.

To join their ranks, you must feel intensely exactly what you plan to make happen — before it happens. You must, as the saying goes, "Sing like you don't need the money." You must not only know your goal, but also be willing to live it so completely that it's a foregone conclusion.

The best way to begin that process, in my experience, is to speak your goal out loud — or write it down and post it in a place where you can see it each and every day. Every truly successful person I've ever met has used one or the other strategy, or both, to regain control of the game when things looked grim.

It's true. The act of speaking your goals out loud — or writing them and posting them in a place where you can see them every day — has a dramatic effect on your ability to attain those goals. Yet many of the people I train get glazed eyes when I start to talk about the importance of focusing on the future in this way, of pulling it into the present by asking themselves, "Where am I going?" and answering the question with conviction.

Perhaps you, too, feel a certain weariness at the prospect of developing a verbal or written summary of what you want from life. I can only respond by saying that I, too, once had a blasé attitude about the importance of living the future in the present by writing down and continually reviewing my goals. Then came the day in the early 1970s when I was lucky enough to be seated next to John Y. Brown II during a long plane flight.

For those of you who aren't familiar with his story, Brown was the man who turned Colonel Harlan Sanders into a national icon. Brown bought Sanders's operation, retained the Colonel as a spokesperson, and launched the global Kentucky Fried Chicken empire. Brown provided the driving force that moved the KFC organization from several hundred to several thousand franchisees, and he is usually considered to be one of the most important figures in sparking the fast-food revolution of the 1970s. In one of the first major transactions of its kind, Brown's group sold the Kentucky Fried Chicken organization to Heublein in 1971 for roughly three and a half times its 1964 purchase price. Brown, who was one of the groundbreaking owners of the American Basketball Association, was also married to former Miss America Phyllis George. At the time I met him, he was preparing to embark on a new phase in his life — a political career. He eventually was elected to the post of governor of Kentucky.

Well, that was the man I found myself sitting next to on my flight. I hope you'll agree with my assessment that my traveling companion knew something about the art of making great things happen.

Shortly after I took my seat, Brown and I exchanged introductions. We chatted for a while. I quickly realized that I was seated next to the most confident person I had ever encountered, and I decided to take advantage of my advantages. I asked him point-blank: "What's your secret? How do you keep yourself focused?" I asked this because I was genuinely curious, and because I wanted to follow whatever strategies for success John Y. Brown could pass along.

The words were hardly off my lips before Brown pulled out a business card — torn and frayed at the edges — that had apparently served as the starting and ending point of his day for some years. On it were written, in a very few words, Brown's major life goals. He showed it to me and said: "Get your big goals down on paper and start living right inside them. Look at your big goals every single day, without fail. Assume they're unfolding for you. They will."

I can't tell you what the items on the card were, because I honestly don't remember any more. What I do remember, however, was the sheer fatigue that small card showed. It was obviously something Brown had returned to time and time again — the "true north" of this man's life compass. Here, I thought to myself, was the future set out on a tiny scrap of paper. Here was a man who not only knew exactly where he was going, but had mastered the art of acting as though he'd already arrived.

> *The only goal you cannot achieve is the one you have not yet recognized.*

I had decided to ask this remarkable role model for advice. I wanted to know precisely how he'd built the life he wanted. He'd told me. Now the question was: Was I going to follow this man's lead, or wasn't I?

I've got a card of my own now. I look at it each and every day. Ever since that encounter with John Y. Brown II, I've made myself a pledge to get specific about all my major goals, and to review both my goals and my action plans for carrying them out constantly. And by constantly, I mean daily. The growth experienced by my organization would not have been possible if I hadn't (1) gotten excited about goals and (2) constantly reminded myself to focus on where I was going, not on the obstacles that faced me in any given moment. (By the way, if you feel your goals and priorities need revision or clarification, you'll find some great ideas under Rule 21.) It's easy to look at what doesn't work and become fixated on obstacles. It takes a little more practice to become a master of possibility. Give yourself that practice.

Choose goals that inspire you. Then constantly remind yourself where you're going. Train yourself to come back to your goals again and again, so you can start acting where you want to be — not where you are. This is a prerequisite to building new business relationships with other people. If you don't learn to act like you're already where you want to be, you won't inspire those who come in contact with you — and you'll have a much harder time winning commitments to action!

MAKE IT HAPPEN PRINCIPLE 3

You can act as though you've already attained your goals by committing them to writing — and reinforcing them verbally every single day.

RULE 4
Focus with Specificity on Your Next Step

One day, a salesperson came back to our office from a meeting with a new prospect. His manager asked him, "How did the meeting go?" The salesperson explained that the rapport had been great, and that the chemistry had been perfect. Then the manager asked, "When are you going back?" The salesperson said, "Actually, the meeting went so well, and my contact learned so much, that he said he never had to meet with me again."

Was the salesperson right? Was that really a great meeting?

Actually, that salesperson had no specific action planned with the other person. In the terminology of our company, he had no Next Step, and therefore he had no prospect.

It's much too common for people to leave a meeting thinking, "That went very well," but to have no idea whether anything will actually take place in the future as a result. Before we walk in the door for a meeting, we have to ask ourselves:

- Where does this relationship stand now?
- Where do I want this relationship to be when the discussion is over?
- What am I going to do to make that happen?

At our company, we ask those questions of ourselves constantly — in part because we know we're going to be asked questions about our contacts! Our managers are focused obsessively on a couple of critical questions about each and every new contact made by employees — whether that contact is a prospective customer, an applicant for a job, a potential business ally, or any other promising new acquaintance. Our managers want to know:

- What happened at the meeting?
- What's happening next on their end?
- When are you going back?

If nothing happened at the meeting, nothing is happening next on the contact's end, and there are no plans to go back, then guess what? We don't consider the person we just met to be worth spending a lot of time and energy on!

> *If you don't have a Next Step, you have nothing.*

For our salespeople, a contact without a Next Step cannot be categorized as an active prospect. You'll get a better sense of what that means when you read Rule 37. Right now, understand that unless there is a Next Step scheduled with a prospective customer, no income can be forecast as coming from that customer. It doesn't matter how "great" the meeting was, how much money the person anticipated spending, how extraordinary the chemistry was, how much you had in common with the person you just met, or how "interested" that person claimed to be in talking to you further. If there's no mutually agreed upon Next Step, it's not a prospect.

The same principle applies to contacts developed in a *nonsales* setting. In our organization, if we want to consider the relationship "active" — if it's going to constitute something on the to-do list of any of our employees — there had better be a reciprocal commitment from the other person we're talking to. Are we meeting next Tuesday at one? Checking in for a conference call first thing Friday morning? Getting an update by e-mail tomorrow morning? Great! Has the other person told us he plans to "connect some time next week or the week after"? Either we make something happen or we take it off the to-do list.

Actions speak louder than words. People who make things happen don't invest time, effort, or energy where there is no reciprocal investment.

So ask the hard questions: In any given situation, what's the Next Step you're planning to ask for? What direct steps will you take to make that happen? What are you prepared to suggest directly to the other person? What ball are you going to throw out?

Consider these two end-of-meeting requests:

"I think this meeting has gone really well. What I want to do is get you a chance to meet the president of our organization and see what our operation looks like. Are you available to take a tour of our facility next Tuesday at three?"

"I think this meeting has gone really well. Can I call you next week?"

Which option throws out the ball? Which is more likely to make something happen in the relationship?

Remember: If there is no commitment to future action at a specific time, or if you're talking to someone who cannot make the decision to work with you, then you have nothing. You have less than nothing. You have a first appointment you're not sure about!

I tell my salespeople that anyone can get in for a first appointment. The trick is to get the other person to agree to meet you a second time! What's worse than not getting the second appointment? *Not knowing* whether you're going to get it!

So ask. Ask directly for the next meeting before you leave the first meeting. Pull out your calendar and suggest a specific date and time. Throw the ball! If you find that the person doesn't throw it back, at least you've made the move.

By preparing to ask for the second meeting at the end of the first meeting, you'll find out exactly where you stand with the other person. Typically, you'll also cut between one and three weeks off the time it takes to get a positive outcome in the relationship.

This point is incredibly important, so forgive me if I repeat it: The minute you walk in the door, you should know what Next Step you plan to ask for. If you make a habit of moving the relationship forward in this way, you will get in the habit of making good things happen in your life and your career.

Don't just tell the boss you want to talk about a raise. Ask if you can discuss your salary review on Monday at 10:00 a.m. If that time isn't free, offer another one!

Don't just ask the prospect you've spoken to for the last three weeks, "Where do we go from here?" Say, "This really makes sense to me. Why don't we get our people in here next week, start developing the program for you, and deliver it on April 6? Does that make sense to you?" (That's exactly what our organization did with a major prospect that had been "on the edge" about whether to work with us. The client went ahead with a series of programs worth well over $100,000!)

MAKE IT HAPPEN PRINCIPLE 4

Every promising meeting, call, or exchange should conclude with you asking for a specific Next Step.

RULE 5   Create a Sense of Urgency

Hollywood agent "Swifty" Lazar often told a story about movie mogul Sam Goldwyn. In the late 1950s, according to Lazar, Goldwyn welshed on a $400,000 verbal agreement to buy the movie rights to Max Shulman's book *Rally Round the Flag, Boys*. Suddenly, Lazar had no deal. He fixed the problem at a party at Frank Sinatra's house by spreading word among two studio heads in attendance that they had to read the book quickly, because (in Lazar's words), "I'm selling the book tomorrow."

Was it a bluff? Was it a prophecy? Who can say? One thing is certain, however. Both studio heads dashed out the door to head home and read the book. Sinatra was miffed that Lazar's ploy caused the early departures. All the same, Lazar did in fact get an offer on *Rally Round the Flag, Boys* the very next day.

Why do you imagine Lazar was so eager to impress on his prospective buyers the importance of acting right away to secure the rights to the novel? Why was he hoping to get a commitment for action in the short term?

You can probably find the answer in your own personal calendar. If you're like most people, your schedule for the next two weeks is blocked in much more heavily than the period that follows.

That's not to say that there's never anything worth scheduling for a month or two down the line. But the period we all tend to pay the closest attention to is the two weeks right in front of us. In fact, it's common for people to schedule less important activities for further out than two weeks, because they believe that they'll have more time then. But what happens? When the event actually comes within the two-week "event horizon," it has to compete with more important commitments — and it gets rescheduled for the following month.

Most experienced businesspeople learn to anticipate this pattern. When someone agrees to meet with me for the first time, and then tries to set a date that's six or eight weeks in the future, my sensors go up. I try to find a way to make the meeting happen sooner. If I can't find a way to move the date up, I'll still schedule the appointment, but I won't be surprised if it drops out of my calendar.

> *People live two weeks at a time.*

Over the years, I've learned what Lazar surely knew — that people live two weeks at a time. Marketers (among many others) have also noticed this fact. Designers of direct mail pieces, for instance, live and die by creating a sense of urgency with their prospects. ("Act now!" "Return this postpaid card before Decmber 16!" "To reserve your free gift, call the toll-free number today!") Lazar, though, may well have been the master at creating "buzz" that made people want to talk to him now, today — before lunch, if possible! Making something happen means getting people to play ball with you — immediately, if possible, but at any rate at some point within the next two weeks.

Actions really do speak louder than words. Swifty Lazar, like most successful people, understood that real interest expresses itself through immediate action — and action, in turn, often inspires interest. By the same token, action *deferred* is usually impossible to distinguish from inaction!

Imagine someone telling you, "I'm fascinated. I'd really like to work with you. Let's get together to talk about this in more detail. How's January of the year 2024?" That's ridiculous, isn't it? Well, that response is only a slightly more obvious variation of a much more common delaying tactic: "That sounds fascinating. Why don't you call me next month so we can talk about it?"

So what does all this mean? It means that getting a Next Step to take place within the next two weeks — or sooner — is much more meaningful than getting a Next Step that may (or may not) take place "sometime next month," or six months from now, or "when the busy season is over." When it comes to evaluating opportunities, sooner is almost always better, and you want to spend most of your available time on the better opportunities! Now, I'm not saying there's no way to work with business clients in the long term. But I am saying that doing business — whether you're selling something, recruiting a new employee for your company, or establishing an important new business alliance with another organization — is a lot like fishing. You're likelier to get what you want when the line is taut than when it's slack.

When you directly suggest a specific action step for sometime within the next two weeks, you tug at the line. When someone agrees to an action step within the next two weeks, the line stays taut. It is in your best interests, whenever you can, to take action to move your Next Step into the window of the next two weeks — and to avoid getting distracted by people whose "interest" doesn't take the form of action within that time frame.

Be like Swifty. Build interest and action in the short term — not "someday." If you mean to get something accomplished, make a habit of taking action to win a slot in people's calendars within that "next two weeks" time frame.

MAKE IT HAPPEN PRINCIPLE 5

Because people live two weeks at a time, a commitment to action in the short term is more significant than a commitment to action in the long term.

6   People Respond in Kind

Like anyone who sells for a living, I encounter my fair share of brush-offs. One of the most common occurs when I reach a president or CEO. The morning that I began work on this chapter, for instance, I made a cold call and connected with the president of a *Fortune* 1000 financial services company. I followed the four-part calling script that you'll read about under Rule 26. After a minute or so, I got to the point in the call where I typically ask for a face-to-face meeting. Here's what I said, confidently and enthusiastically:

> "Mr. Prospect, the reason I'm calling you today specifically is to set an appointment so we can talk about the success we've had with XYZ Company. I'd really like to get together with you to talk about what we were able to do for them. How's Tuesday at three?"

Notice what I didn't say to the prospect. I didn't ask whether he'd "like" to get together. I didn't ask what he "thought about" the idea of meeting with me. And I didn't ask "what time was good" for him to schedule a meeting. ("Is Tuesday morning better for you, or Wednesday afternoon?") I certainly didn't ask whether he "felt comfortable working with a company like ours."

Those are all very common approaches people use when reaching out to new contacts. Stop and think for a moment. Are they really the topics you want to introduce in a discussion with a new contact? Look at the various possibilities I had with my prospect. What's likely to happen in any of these scenarios?

Possible Subjects to Discuss with Head of Fortune 1000 Financial Firm

1. Whether he'd like to get together. (Considering the history of our relationship — approximately 90 seconds — the prospect may well view this request as presumptuous. How can he "like" the idea of meeting someone he didn't know before he picked up the phone?)

2. What he thinks of the possibility of a meeting. (When new contacts ask me this on the phone, I'm tempted to answer, "Do you really *want* to know what I'm thinking?")

3. The time of day that is typically best for him. (Theoretically, this could lead to extended philosophical discussion of the contact's daily and weekly workflow patterns: "You know, I never thought about that before. Which is better — I mean in a fundamental sense? Is Tuesday more secure from an epistemological point of view, or is it Wednesday?")

4. Whether he feels comfortable working with a company like our company. (It's a little early in the relationship to be asking questions like this — so early, in fact that my chance of receiving an accurate answer is virtually nil. See Rule 40 for a more detailed discussion of how to be sure you get the right information as the relationship progresses.)

5. Whether he can meet with me Tuesday afternoon at three to talk about what we did for XYZ Company. (That's what I'm most interested in finding out about at this stage in the relationship.)

I didn't raise items 1 through 4. I was interested in item 5. I wanted to find out whether the prospect and I could get together Tuesday at three. So I made a conscious choice to point the entire exchange toward that narrowly defined subject.

Suddenly, "Tuesday at three" was under discussion. And sure enough, that's what my contact responded to.

Do you know what he said? After a longish pause he told me, "Steve, Tuesday really wouldn't work for me." What just happened? Suddenly, my new contact and I were talking about *when* our meeting would take place, rather than *whether* it would take place. I suggested another date and time. We set the appointment.

People respond in kind. Use that information to your benefit — and make conscious choices about the subjects of the interactions you engage in! Think about this: *People who let others determine the focus let others control their lives.* If you're going to make something happen before lunch, you have to do what it takes to maintain your own focus and your own attitude during any given exchange. The subject you choose will affect the response you hear. Just as important, the attitude you choose — enthusiastic, depressed, grateful, cynical, supremely confident — will also affect what you hear in response. If I make a call and sound petulant, rude, or angry, the content of the message probably won't matter. My conversational partner will simply respond to the negative emotions I've sent out.

By consciously choosing a subject and an emotional tone, you can control the flow of any exchange.

That call I made to the Fortune 1000 CEO is only one illustration of how this powerful principle works. The same idea has applications in virtually every aspect of business life. For instance, if I'm working with a key vendor who's supplying a critical piece of equipment for an upcoming program of ours, I can raise the issue of time in a number of different ways. I can say, "Todd, what does your capacity look like in the shop this month?" Or I can say, "Todd, what can we do to get this project in our warehouse by the fifteenth of next month?" With the second approach, I've thrown the ball out to Todd in a very direct and specific way. I'm controlling the conversation. I'm giving Todd something concrete to respond to.

Is it possible Todd could tell me that the fifteenth is impossible? Is it possible my prospect will tell me that he has no interest whatsoever in meeting with me? Certainly! But the sooner I know about those reactions, the better. At least I've thrown the ball out — and avoided wasting a lot of time dealing in abstractions.

Very often, when I reach the head of a company, I'll get this kind of response:

> "Steve, that sounds fascinating, but the truth is, I don't handle this directly. You need to check in with the Vice President of Such and Such, Joe Smith. You can tell him I said for you to give him a call."

Most businesspeople, in such a situation, will simply call up Joe Smith and say:

> "Joe Smith? Hi, this is Janet Brown, and, uh, President Bigshot suggested that I give you a call . . ."

The minute the other person hears that, what's the response? I don't know about you, but most of the people I talk to tell me that when they get a call like that, their first thought is, "Here we go again. Bigshot is pawning off another one of his calls on me. This should be boring."

Instead of leading with the implied topic, "Mr. Bigshot didn't have time for this," I give the person something very different to respond to. Here's what I say, in a tone of voice that fairly radiates enthusiasm:

> "Hi — Joe Smith? Steve Schiffman here, with D.E.I. Management Group. Did Mr. Bigshot tell you I'd be calling?"

By choosing my topic carefully, I've gotten the conversation off to a very different start indeed! Now we're talking about *whether* Mr. Bigshot mentioned the call. That's a much better subject, as far as I'm concerned! The person starts thinking: "Did Mr. Bigshot mention Schiffman? Was I supposed to be ready for this call? After all, it sounds important." Well, guess what? This call *is* important!

You have no idea how smoothly the conversation flows, how receptive the other person usually is, when you use an opening like this. But you have to choose to use it. You have to *decide* what topic you want the other person to respond to.

I'll be coming back to this idea of controlling the flow of a conversation at various points throughout the book, because it's a vitally important concept. For now, just remember that people respond in kind to the subjects we raise. If we ask about the weather, they generally don't start talking immediately about quantum theory. What's more, if we show enthusiasm and optimism, they tend to respond more enthusiastically and optimistically to us.

MAKE IT HAPPEN PRINCIPLE 6

You can control the flow of any interaction by deciding ahead of time what you want people to respond to.

RULE 7

Understand That People Communicate in Stories

Some years back, the late columnist Jim Bishop wrote a piece about how tired he'd grown of people asking "What's up?" or "How are things going?" without really listening to his answers. One acquaintance in particular made a habit of calling him, asking how he was, and then instantly steamrolling past any response Bishop made.

One morning, Bishop decided to find out just how bad his contact's listening skills really were. After the fellow launched another call with his usual "Hey, Jim, how are you?" opening, Bishop said, "I've got lung cancer."

"That's great" was the immediate response. "Say, Jim . . . "

Sometimes, we ignore other people's stories at our peril. By the same token, eliciting stories — and listening to them with full attention — is an essential success strategy.

Once you get someone to share a story with you, you have a better idea of that person's priorities and world view. Stories give you invaluable information and insight in virtually any business situation. Consider the job interview. I talk to many prospective employees over the course of a year. Recently I had the opportunity to interview an applicant who appeared to have all the right credentials on her résumé. She had experience selling in an industry that was related to ours, and she had a record of increasingly impressive achievement as a salesperson. The question was: Was she right for our organization? In other words, did this alliance make sense for both sides?

During the course of my interview with the applicant, I asked a simple open-ended question: "Can you tell me

29

what it was like to work for your last employer?" In doing this, I was subtly inviting the applicant to tell me a story. Here's what I heard:

> "Well, I guess the main problem was with my supervisor. He had real difficulty with creative people. He insisted on micromanaging me; if you didn't do things exactly his way, he would get paranoid about your work. For instance, you couldn't just call customers and referrals. You had to call people you'd *never spoken to before,* and you had to do it between eight and nine o'clock in the morning. I tried to tell him that there were a lot of ways to get sales, not just his way. We tried to clear the air, and then he got transferred to another division of the company. The new manager who came in was more understanding of what it's like to sell face to face. He and I got along a lot better."

I'm paraphrasing the answer slightly, of course, but that's basically what I got from the other side of the desk. How would you interpret the story I heard? Here were a couple of things I picked up. First of all, I'd asked, "what it was like to work" for an employer, and the applicant started talking about "problems." Then there was the applicant's ominous decision to speak poorly of a former supervisor — without my having encouraged her in any way to do so! Even more alarming was the applicant's resistance to any kind of prospecting system or regimen; if the last manager couldn't get this "creative" sales rep to reach out to new people to set appointments, what were our odds of being able to point her in that direction?

Despite the applicant's record of stellar achievement, I decided that she was probably better off on her own or with another company. By persuading her to tell me a story, I was able to get a look at her world view — and save myself (and her) a great deal of exasperation down the line. I can't tell you how many applicants have helped me come to a quick decision by sharing a story that demonstrated clearly that they had a world view that wouldn't fit in at our company. (For instance, I've run into applicants whose stories convinced me that they were angry at the world; that they were experts at pinning blame on others; that they did not make decisions well independently; and so on.)

If a story convinces you that there is a very low or nonexistent chance for a mutually beneficial relationship, thank the person for his or her time and move on to someone else.

The same strategy works if I want to learn more about a prospective customer. When I meet a new contact at a business my company hasn't worked with before, I ask questions like these:

- How did you get this job?
- What were you doing before that?
- How did the company get started?

Without fail, the person will open up and start telling me a story. It could be a story about his or her career, or it could be one that shows me exactly what the contact's priorities are on the job. Whatever it is, the story is going to give me a glimpse of the way that individual looks at the world, and it's going to give me an idea about how (or whether) the two of us can work together profitably.

Everybody communicates in stories. Every story has a point. Every story tells you something about the priorities of the person you're talking to.

> *Elicit stories to find out what is important to the other person. This is crucial to establishing a good business relationship.*

31

Of course, any business discussion is a matter of balance. If all you do is listen, without contributing anything meaningful of your own, the conversation won't go well. If, on the other hand, you fail to explore a statement like "I've got lung cancer" or "There are big changes on the horizon for our company," you'll lose points. Keep everything in perspective.

The questions I've mentioned in this chapter are excellent ways to encourage stories, but very often you'll find that little or no encouragement is necessary! When you're visiting with new contacts, and you ask what they're trying to get accomplished, listen closely to the answer. You may well find that your contact concludes by telling you a story. Let them. Don't cut them off. Follow their lead. They'll start telling stories that illustrate exactly what they're trying to accomplish in their job, in their career, in their business. If you use that information correctly, you can build bridges that benefit both of you.

Encourage people to tell you their stories. Then listen attentively, and act intelligently on what you hear. Ask how people found themselves in a certain situation; ask why a certain event was important to them. (See Rule 34 for more on the importance of "how" and "why" questions.)

Eliciting stories is the very best way to get a fuller understanding of what people do, how they do it, when they do it, where they do it, who they do it with, and why they choose to do it a certain way. Then, and only then, can you decide whether there's a chance for you to act on what you've heard to help them do what they do better.

MAKE IT HAPPEN PRINCIPLE 7

By eliciting stories, you can encourage people to tell you what's happened to them, and why it's important.

8   Expect Negative
Initial Responses

There's a woman in Canada who's taken our training program and applied it to her phone prospecting work. She takes any negative response she gets from a contact and uses it as a transition to schedule an appointment. If the person says, "I can't meet with you, I have no money," she says, "You know what? I think that's why we really ought to get together. How's Tuesday at two?" If the person says, "I don't know anything about your firm," she says, "You know what? I think that's why we really ought to get together. How's Tuesday at two?" If the person says, "We had a really horrible experience with your company the last time around, she says, "You know what? I think that's why we really ought to get together. How's Tuesday at two?"

That may be a little brusque, and though the spirit is right, it's not exactly the turnaround approach we recommend. (You'll find out about turnarounds under Rule 27.) But the truth is that what this salesperson does works for her. She sets an incredible number of appointments that way. The reason? She understands the purpose of her call. She's not flustered when she gets resistance from a new contact. Her aim is to get the response out on the table so she can deal with it directly and attempt to set up a meeting.

Is that why you're calling someone? Or are you thrown when you hear resistance from someone you've never spoken to before?

Whether or not you sell for a living, the telephone is a tool of incredible potential power. And anyone who must set face-to-face meetings with new contacts can tap into that power.

Think about it. Imagine we want to meet with John Smith. If we reach Smith by phone, we can instantly change his priorities, at least for a moment. Suppose Smith is working on a crossword puzzle. To him, the crossword puzzle is the most important thing in the world at that moment. Then the phone rings. Reluctantly, Smith answers it. Maybe there's an emergency! For the next few seconds, the most important thing in the world to John Smith is — whatever's about to come out of that telephone.

That's an awesome power. But what do we do with the attention we get in those first few seconds? Are we going to be thrown when we get a negative response from Smith when he realizes that, once he gets off the phone with us, he can get back to that crossword puzzle? Is that really going to be a major surprise to us?

By choosing the topic, we can control the flow. (See Rule 6.) But even if we've pointed the conversation toward a topic we like, we're going to encounter negative responses. After a while, it's not going to surprise us when people say, "I have no interest." Ideally, we may prefer a response like "Boy, am I glad you called" from John Smith. But in the real world, we know that's not what we're usually going to hear. Instead, we're going to meet some resistance.

And that's okay. Because we're going to be ready for the responses we get. We're going to anticipate them. We're not going to let them throw us. Just like that salesperson in Canada, we're going to stay focused and resume our conversation.

Please understand that *any time* you suggest something new to someone you don't yet know well, there's going to be some initial resistance. You'll be in a much better position to make something happen in any new relationship if you accept that the goal of your first call or discussion with a new contact must be to get that negative response out in the open — not to avoid it.

> *People who make things happen are messengers of change. They try to get initial negative responses out on the table early, so they can address them directly.*

Why is any of this important? Because time is so precious. If we hem and haw on the phone, we'll waste John Smith's time and attention — and lose our opportunity.

In any early discussion with a new contact, our mindset has to be that we are not selling our product or service, not selling our company to a bank officer, not selling our department to a potential star employee. Instead, we are selling an appointment — and any sale has a selling cycle. So assume we're making initial contact with a new person over the phone. In this case, I can tell you that the selling cycle for making an appointment over the phone is typically one to three minutes. That's not much time! In this very abbreviated conversation, we want to control the flow by making the appointment the topic of conversation — and we want to get that initial resistance response out in the open so we can deal with it.

Again: In any appointment call that exceeds three minutes, we are less likely to get an appointment than we are in a shorter call. Beyond three minutes, we either are "explaining" too much to someone we don't yet know a lot about, or we're getting beaten up, and wasting our time trying to counterpunch. Neither approach is productive.

Instead, we want to follow the example of that lady in Canada. We want to get the negative response out on the table and try to deal with it. Unfortunately, this is the exact opposite of the approach many people take. ("Maybe if I talk fast enough, the prospect will agree to meet with me.") The whole purpose of the call is to get an initial response that we can work with. And usually, that initial response is negative.

Now, the good news is that we can easily anticipate all the various negative responses and develop effective strategies for turning them around. Believe it or not, these responses all fall into one of five categories, which we will discuss under Rule 27.

The bad news is that these negative responses come at us very fast, just like a 90-mile-per-hour fastball. That's why appointment making is such a hard game at first.

With practice, though, it can become very easy — as long as you understand that getting this kind of Next Step over the phone is not an intellectual skill. You can't expect to be so persuasive in your initial minute that you "convince" the person not to put up any resistance whatsoever.

Instead, setting appointments by phone is a verbal game of catch. You have to be fast with that game of catch, but once you understand it, you can master it by controlling the flow of the conversation and anticipating that there will be negative responses.

MAKE IT HAPPEN PRINCIPLE 8

The purpose of the appointment-setting call is to produce a response that you can deal with; initially, that response is likely to be negative.

RULE 9 Know Where You Add Value

I once had a brainstorm that was so great it nearly bankrupted me. In fact, if my concept hadn't been quite so good, I wouldn't have found myself facing the worst financial crisis of my life.

In 1984, I came up with an idea that was strong enough to convince me that I could ignore my training business. All that really mattered, I told myself, was "working the kinks" out of my breakthrough new idea. These days, I will certainly try out new ideas — but I can promise you that there will never be another working day in my life when I forget to work in an area that I *know from experience* I can use to add value to someone else's operation.

What was the idea that broke my routine? Well, at the time, very few of the thousands of doctors' offices in Manhattan did their billing through a computer system. The invoices and envelopes were hand-typed; the payments were usually hand-entered into some old-fashioned paper and ink ledger. There was, I knew, a huge emerging market for software that could streamline the operations of these physicians' offices. A doctor colleague of mine and I decided that we could become instant software experts. He promised to put up a large sum of money, and I decided to write the business plan. We signed papers and started a company.

Here's what I told myself at the time: "What I'm developing is so new, so exciting, so important, that I can skip my hour of daily calls to new training contacts for a little while." Never mind that training had a demonstrated capacity to pay my bills. Never mind that the new idea was something I had no experience in. This was important!

"If my idea is good enough," I thought, "and if I can execute it, I'll more than make up for any lost time. This business is going to be incredibly successful. The training business will always be there for me after I set the computer business up."

So it was that I decided to ignore my proven market. I tracked down the technical people and the lawyers and the accountants, and focused exclusively on logistical questions for several months. I stopped reaching out to new people. I stopped making calls. I stopped focusing on making new connections happen in the area where I knew I could add value. I stopped devoting myself to what I did best. (A side note: By talking myself out of making any calls whatsoever to new people who could use what I had to offer, I was also breaking Rule 24, which you'll be reading about a little later.)

I started focusing obsessively on a "quick hit" business I knew virtually nothing about and didn't believe in at a gut level. I was going to start up this business in a field in which I had little actual interest and zero expertise, sell the systems myself, and dominate the new market in a year or so — before selling out at a handsome profit. All I had to do was find out what the software had to do, hire the programmers, and talk to the attorneys and accountants. In no time, I told myself, I'd have the whole thing set up.

Surprise, surprise: There were some delays. A couple of months down the line, my partner got cold feet. "I'm a doctor," he said, "not a computer guy." At the time, I was furious, but looking back, I can understand his viewpoint. When he backed out, the financing he'd promised me evaporated. I couldn't pay my programmers — or anyone else.

> *If you don't believe deeply in the value of what
> you're doing, why bother?*

The doctor and I eventually worked out a settlement, but the partial payment he sent along still left me deeply in debt. I had no product to show for all my work. And — most distressing of all — I had no training business on the horizon!

Focusing exclusively on the logistics related to my new idea was the worst decision of my career. The problem wasn't that our idea hadn't been good. It had been *great*. We had been absolutely right. Doctors *were* eventually going to start using this technology. But, as it turned out, we weren't the people to get the computers and the software up and running for them!

The tricky thing about great ideas is that they often distract us. The greater they are, the more distracting they can be. Sometimes, of course, it pays to be a *little* distracted by a great idea. I've learned from bitter experience, though, that it doesn't make sense to get *so* obsessed with the technical issues connected to any exciting idea that you stop talking to people about what you know already works.

Mistakes are, of course, how we learn. The biggest lesson I learned from this experience, however, was not that I wasn't cut out to be a high-tech entrepreneur. The real lesson I picked up was this: No idea is great enough to justify, for even a single day, completely neglecting proven, revenue-generating activities.

I didn't realize it at the time, but when I decided not to make my daily calls to talk to people about what I *already knew I could do,* I was riding for a fall. When the money dried up and the project fell through, I had no training dates scheduled and absolutely no income on the horizon. (To find out how I pulled myself out of this particular tailspin, see Rule 10.)

Don't let what happened to me happen to you. Review your daily schedule closely. If it doesn't include some kind of activity that you *know for certain adds value to the day of someone else,* revise the schedule.

MAKE IT HAPPEN PRINCIPLE 9

If a great idea causes you to stop talking to people about what you already do well, you're asking for trouble.

RULE 10 No Contact Base Is Big Enough

After a failed attempt in the mid-1980s to turn myself into a computer software entrepreneur, I faced a daunting challenge: How do I move from having absolutely no business scheduled to having some billable business this week? This was quite a challenge, because everything I had ever learned (or trained anyone) about selling told me that I was looking at bankruptcy.

I didn't just need a big training date — I needed a big training date that started immediately, because I had let my prospecting lapse for months. Understand: My sales cycle was approximately eight weeks. That is to say, it took me an average of two months to turn a new contact into a customer. I now had absolutely nothing — zero — on the calendar, and no one even considering me for a training date. Just to keep things consistent, I had absolutely nothing in the bank. That meant that, if I picked up the phone that morning and managed to strike up a decent conversation with someone who wanted to talk to me about training, I could expect to wait for eight weeks before signing a contract that carried any kind of up-front fee.

The problem was, I didn't have eight weeks. As a matter of fact, if the process took any longer than a week, I didn't even have a phone number. (The bill for my two lines, alas, was well overdue.) As a practical matter, what I was trying to accomplish seemed extremely close to impossible.

And yet I felt I had to try. The way I saw it, I had two options. I could do something I really didn't want to do — shut down the business and get a job selling insurance, say — or I could find some way to get myself past this crisis within the next week by securing an assignment with a half-on-signing fee attached to it. Even though all my experience told me that the second option was impossible, I decided I had to find some way to get my business out of the hole.

I thought for hours about the best way to compress an eight-week selling cycle into a single week. After developing a number of less than satisfactory strategies, I decided there was one small chance. To take advantage of it, I would have to take something I knew full well worked in small doses — telephone prospecting — and apply it in very, very large doses.

"My best shot," I told myself, "is to connect with some large organization that has scheduled a training date with some competitor of mine that has canceled for some reason. If I can fill a slot like that for a large company, I can make it." I didn't know where that large company was, but I felt it had to be out there somewhere, and I resolved to connect with it.

The only way I could imagine doing that was to call vast numbers of businesses and find out exactly what they were currently doing in terms of training. That meant I had to have lots and lots of numbers to call.

"No list of company names is going to be too long for what I have to accomplish," I thought to myself. "I'm going to have to find a whole lot of leads to call, and I'm going to have to do that, flat out, for a very long time." No matter how many people I already had on my list to call, I felt I needed more.

I locked myself in my office over a long Labor Day weekend and wrote down the names and numbers of everyone I could think of who had even a tangential connection to anyone with a business or charitable organization that might be working with outside trainers. I burrowed through business directories. I circled every relevant business mentioned in all the newspapers at my disposal. These days, you can use the Internet to develop a lead list. Back then, I had a pen, a couple of directories, a pile of newspapers, and a yellow legal pad. I made the most of them.

> *Losses occur. Keep them in perspective and move on to the next new business relationship.*

I wrote down the names of hundreds of people and companies, and I taped all the yellow sheets to the walls of my office. Early Tuesday morning, after the Labor Day holiday had passed, I started calling that list, finding out exactly what kind of training people were doing and asking for referrals at every turn. Now, typically, I make 15 cold calls a day, and I complete that work in an hour or so. (See Rule 24.) On this occasion, I made calls for two solid days.

At the end of the second day, an amazing thing happened. I got a call back from someone who informed me that, yes, a sales trainer who was scheduled to give a program had canceled unexpectedly. Was I available on short notice?

I took a deep breath and told my contact that I'd check my calendar. Then I informed her that, yes, we could probably work something out.

I hope and pray that you never have to go through that kind of experience. Whether or not you do, however, you should know this: When you take control of your plan to initiate contact with new people, you control your own destiny. I believe you can make *any* kind of professional relationship happen that you need to make happen — if you are willing to do the right work up front. Under ordinary circumstances, compressing the sales cycle from eight weeks to one week is virtually impossible. But it turned out that there was a way to compress that cycle, and that way involved massively expanding my list of leads.

That one training engagement got my business over the hump. Now, years after the crisis, my company has trained nearly 600,000 people, opened offices in multiple cities, and done business with some of the biggest companies in the country. Everything we do now, though, is rooted in a direct, personal understanding of the simple principle that allowed me to resurrect my business: Virtually anything is possible if you've still got a live dial tone — and if you assume that your list of contacts can always be expanded. It can!

MAKE IT HAPPEN PRINCIPLE 10

You can accomplish just about anything if you assume that no contact base is big enough — and constantly expand your pool of possible contacts.

11 Know Your Personal Commercial

"So — where do you work?"
"What do you do for a living?"
"Tell me about yourself."

Those are the kinds of questions a brokerage professional I'll call Martin found himself facing over and
over again during a big, glittery party thrown to benefit a
worthy charity he supported. How would you have
responded if you had been in Martin's position?

Would you have said, "Oh, I work for XYZ Company.
How about you?"

Would you have said, "I handle stock transactions. It's
not really that interesting."

Would you have said, "I'm a senior investment coun-
selor. That's the formal title, anyway."

Here's the most important question. Would you have
improvised each response? In other words, would you
have said something different to each person who asked
you?

If you stop and think about what you've done in the
past two weeks or so, you'll probably be able to come up
with at least one example of a social gathering at which
you were asked a question similar to the ones Martin
faced. Someone, at some point, asked you a question that
gave you an opportunity to spotlight *what you do* and
why you do it. What an opportunity! When people ask
questions like that, they're throwing a conversational

"ball" your way. Why not throw it back in a consistent way that briefly explains what you're excited about in your life?

Just as we can expect *negative* responses from the people we interact with, we can anticipate *openings*. We can *make something happen* — that is, move the relationship forward — if we are ready to respond instantly with a short personal commercial that emphasizes what we do to add value to other people's days. The important word here is *short*.

Here's what Martin said to all the people who threw the ball *his* way during that party:

> "I work for ABC Brokerage Company. Basically, my specialty is helping high-net-worth investors make their money work more efficiently. I connect with a lot of entertainers and senior executives, and I help them design large-scale portfolios that match their objectives. My goal is to set up plans that will increase people's net worth, even while they're sleeping."

That's Martin's personal commercial. It's not overbearing. It comes out very naturally, very spontaneously. And it's *true*! It describes exactly what Martin does during the day without apology or hesitation.

Martin has practiced this short statement hundreds if not thousands of times. It's practically a mantra for him. Anyone who asks Martin where he works or what he does for a living, anyone who says, "Tell me about yourself," will hear that answer.

Having a personal commercial is a great way to move relationships forward. Just ask Martin. At that party, dozens of wealthy partygoers *qualified themselves* by asking him to go into more detail about his work with ABC Brokerage Company. Three of those partygoers ended up deciding on their own to do business with Martin. The combined net worth of these three new clients was well over $100 million!

Do you have a personal commercial? Do you have a short, compelling answer to questions like "What do you do?" and "Can you tell me about yourself?" You should!

Tell everyone you meet what you do.

Take a few moments now to develop or refine your personal commercial. Once you've done this, ask yourself these questions about the commercial:

1. Is your personal commercial short enough to deliver comfortably in a social setting in 30 seconds or less? (Be prepared to rewrite and revise your commercial until it sounds natural to your own ear.)

2. Is your commercial casual enough to be delivered conversationally — not as a "hard sell" sales pitch? (Remember, you're talking only about that which you do, not about what you feel you *could* do for the person you're talking to.)

3. Does your commercial focus specifically on how you add value to other people's days? (Think about the problems that would arise during the day if you *didn't* do what you do, and ask yourself how people benefit from actions you undertake.)

If you can honestly answer yes to all three questions, you're ready to "hardwire" your commercial. Practice it over and over again until you can recite it instantly, fluently, and without any embarrassment. Practice smiling as you say it — this will improve your delivery.

If you and I were to meet at a party, and you were to ask me what I did for a living, here's exactly what you'd hear:

> "I'm president of D.E.I. Management Group. We're a sales training firm based in New York City. We help companies improve their performance in the areas of prospect management, appointment making, and high-efficiency selling. We've worked with companies like Motorola, Sprint, Aetna/USHealthcare, and lots of others, and we've trained over half a million people over the past two decades."

Most people do not have a personal commercial. Whether you're an accountant, a salesperson, an entrepreneur, a freelance writer, or a professional dog groomer, you will enhance your contacts with other people once you develop a short statement like the one you just read. Practice yours until you can recite it instantly upon being awakened from a deep sleep. That's important, because we always fall back on that which is familiar to us. (See Rule 12.)

Even in an unfamiliar situation with a person you know nothing about, you must be able to respond quickly and confidently when asked to provide a short biography of yourself. That biography must be brief, must be casual and conversational, and must focus on what you personally *do* to add value.

MAKE IT HAPPEN PRINCIPLE 11

You should be ready to use your
personal commercial in any social situation in which
you're asked a question like "What do you do?"

12 Lie to Your Own Brain— So You Can Hardwire Your Best Moves

If someone were to ask you to name the greatest basketball player in history, what would your answer be? If you're like most people polled in a recent survey, your response would be both immediate and pretty easy to justify: Michael Jordan.

I won't bore you with the mind-bending statistics on the books reflecting Jordan's remarkable career in the National Basketball Association. (If you're a serious basketball fan, you probably know some of them already.) All I want to do is remind you that Air Jordan so dominated his chosen field of endeavor that people who know next to nothing about sports can divide the modern basketball era into two periods: Before Michael and After Michael. Thanks to the magic of videotape, we've all seen him defy gravity in slow motion in countless impossible slamdunks. We've all seen him fake defenders out of their shoes. We've all seen him drain last-minute clutch shots that won games — and championships.

How does mastery on such an awesome level take root? Some people point to Jordan's legendary tenacity and will to win. (One of my favorite quotes from His Airness is, "If we haven't won yet, I'm not tired.") Others attribute Jordan's greatness to his intensity and mental toughness. Still others say the key to his success was his astonishing physical prowess. For my part, I think all these factors played a role, but I believe something very different — something unique to Jordan — allowed him to exceed the many gifted athletes who competed against him in the NBA. I believe Michael Jordan achieved at the level he did because he made sure, day in and day out, that he was the greatest *practice* player in NBA history.

Here's the next question: How did Jordan *become* the greatest practice player? I have a theory: He regularly *lied* to his own brain about the practices he was attending.

What I mean is this: Jordan routinely fooled himself into believing he wasn't attending practices at all. He treated practices like games that counted in the standings! As a result, Jordan *burned in* his best maneuvers and strategies at a very deep level, because his belief fueled a level of intensity that constantly expanded and reinforced his highest skills.

> *Develop a routine for success and burn it into your mind.*

Everyone acknowledges that Jordan's intensity and competitive spirit during team practices were simply impossible to match. Even a cursory review of the press accounts of his practice habits leads to the conclusion that, during his playing days, Jordan took workouts very seriously, indeed. Consider the following:

> [Jordan's] almost psychotic competitiveness in even the most casual practice situation has caused some strain over the years, much of which has been chronicled in *The Jordan Rules*, the best-seller written by the *Chicago Tribune*'s Sam Smith. But, ultimately, what hath it wrought? A much grittier Chicago team, that's certain.
>
> — Jack McCallum, *Sports Illustrated*, January 23, 1991

[John] Bach was a Chicago assistant during the Bulls' [first] three championship years [1991, '92 and '93], and in practice he would devise schemes designed to stop His

49

Airness. "He'd say, 'What've you got for me today, Johnny? I'm going to whip it,'" says Bach.

— Phil Taylor, *Sports Illustrated*, May 8, 1995

Jordan has been called the best practice player ever. . . . This doesn't mean only the amount of time he spends practicing. This means that he practices harder than anyone else during practice. He performs each drill as if he was really in a game. By practicing this way, he prepares himself to react at game speed every time. That way when he encounters that situation in a game, he already knows how to react to it.

— excerpt from an article on www.basketballpro.com, February 2000

Jordan works so hard even in practice, where so many superstars coast, that his teammates have no choice but to push themselves so they won't be embarrassed.

— NBA Web site archive story, 1997 finals coverage

He took pride in his defense. Mike was furious if his teammates didn't play good defense — in practice.

— Ron Coley, former *high school* coach of Jordan's, 1998

I'd pay money to see him practice.

— Larry Brown, San Antonio Spurs coach, January 1999

I always thought Larry [Bird] worked harder than anybody, getting the absolute most from his skills. And back then, I never thought that Michael or anyone could ever be as intense as Larry in terms of winning. But Michael is at least his equal in all those categories, besides being the superior athlete.

— Danny Ainge, former teammate of Larry Bird's, 1999

Top-tier superstars don't wait until a championship is on the line to practice their jump shots. They assume the game really is on the line *as they're practicing*. They trick their brains into believing the drill sessions are the real thing. As a result, they get extraordinary results from their minds and bodies, and a very few — like Jordan — develop an uncommon flexibility that enables them to reinvent themselves over time to adapt to new situations. As Jack McCallum of *Sports Illustrated* put it: "This is a guy who first won championships based on his athletic ability, then he comes back and does it in a whole different way by becoming the smartest player in the league, perhaps the best jump shooter in the league. I think the fact that he did it two different ways and had the chance to come back in a way that no other athlete has done, to me stamps him as the greatest of all time." Who's going to argue that Jordan's practice routine had nothing to do with that transformation?

I use this fool-the-brain principle to develop role-plays and status reviews for our employees that are just as intense as face-to-face meetings with prospects and clients. (Sometimes they may feel even *more* intense.) In fact, the very best salespeople at some of the world's largest companies make a habit of role-playing calls and presentations ahead of time. They do this every day, day in and day out, in a frame of mind I can only describe as 100 percent committed to success. They ask their colleagues and managers to raise the toughest problems and the most challenging responses, so they can practice reacting to them *as though the business were on the line*. That way, when they're facing a similar situation in the real world, they'll be able to respond instinctively and easily.

Here are some other examples of how this burn-it-in idea can be applied.

Walt Disney was famous for his strategy of obsessively "storyboarding" sequences in his animated motion pictures. If you're not familiar with storyboarding or Disney's pioneering role in promoting it as a creative tool, here's a little background. Before assigning his artists, technicians, and performers to begin work on the actual sound or images to be used in a film, Disney would ask key team members to "block out" the high points and pin them on bulletin boards, one after another. That way he and his entire team could review the various shots in the correct order *long before any work began in front of cameras or microphones*. Disney would drill the plan for the sequence over and over in this way.

In other words, *each and every* storyboarded sequence was subjected to intense scrutiny, revision, and discussion *long before the actual "game" of shooting the movie began*. Before anyone actually started executing the plan, Disney would tear the plan apart and put it together again. Before a word of dialogue was recorded, before a note of music was played, before a frame of film was drawn, painted, or shot, Disney wanted a look at a dry run that was so intensely conceived, so deeply thought out, that it might as well have been the movie itself. But it wasn't!

You'll see the same principle applied constantly in the world of politics. Any major candidate for public office eventually has to deal with hostile press conferences, often in front of live television cameras. Now, if you're running for high office, do you wait until the cameras are actually pointed your way to practice your performance? Of course not. Do you simply write down answers to a few likely questions and read your notes over a couple of times before you step in front of the lights? Not if you hope to win! No, you recruit a few of your smartest aides and run a *mock* press conference. You ask your people to hit you with the toughest questions. You tell them to be *tougher* on you than the reporters are likely to be. You treat your practice period just as though it were the event itself, and the closer you come to hitting that standard, the better your performance in front of the reporters is going to be.

So let's recap: In order to perform at peak capacity in an actual game, Jordan fooled his brain into thinking that practices *were* actual games — and hardwired his best moves.

In order to respond professionally and appropriately during sales calls and presentations, the best salespeople engage in intense role-plays that don't just simulate interactions with prospects and customers, but trick the brain into believing it's engaged in an *actual* discussion with a prospective customer. That way top salespeople hardwire their own best questions, comebacks, and turnarounds so they can use them when dollars are at stake.

In order to get his team to execute a sequence of the highest possible quality, Disney made his people act as though they *were* shooting the film when in fact they were sketching it out on sheets of paper — and hardwired the best ideas.

In order to perform well in front of hostile reporters, savvy politicians run mock press conferences and encourage their senior aides to be as rough on them as possible in posing questions. That way, they can hardwire the poise, precision, and master of detail they must have to look good under fire.

A wonderful thing happens when you follow these examples. Once you lie to your brain enough times about whether you're practicing or executing, your brain loses track — and executing at peak level eventually becomes second nature!

My point is *not* that anyone who treats basketball practices like regular-season games can eventually shoot and defend like Michael Jordan on the court. I don't believe that's true! What I'm trying to get across is that *top-tier superstars make a habit of lying to their own*

53

brains. They use intense, emotional repetition in "battlefield conditions" to imprint their best strategies at an extremely deep level of consciousness. And you can too. In fact, you already do something very similar without even realizing it.

Think of a time that you were driving somewhere, and you suddenly saw something in front of you that you didn't expect to see. Haven't you ever had to act quickly to avoid hitting an object in the middle of the road, at least once? Sure you have. Here's a question for you. When that happened, did you have to stop and think about whether it was a good idea for you to step on the brake? Did you think, "Hmm — there's a deer. I wonder what my options are here? Suppose I considered bringing my right foot down sharply on the pedal that controls the braking mechanism of this automobile. What kind of outcome would that produce?"

I hope your answer is no. If you'd been driving for more than a couple of months, you actually had hundreds, probably thousands of braking experiences of various levels of intensity for your brain and body to draw on. As a result, your central nervous system took over automatically. You avoided impact, because your brain had taken the previous braking experiences very seriously indeed.

So here's my question. If you know your body and mind can be programmed in this way just by driving around in a car for a few months, what are you willing to program in *consciously*? In other words: What's important enough for you to decide to treat as a league game?

In challenging situations, human beings inevitably respond with that which is most familiar. That means *we can't afford to wait in order to get the right moves down!* We have to hardwire them so they're second nature to us.

We have to be like Mike. We have to treat the practice as though it's actually a game. We have to approach our drills with near-psychotic intensity. We have to design and critique the storyboard as though we really were shooting the motion picture. We have to subject ourselves to a mock press conference that's just as tough as the real thing. We have to role-play the sales discussion just as though we were face to face with the customer.

Once we use repetition and intensity to fool our minds into believing we're not at practice, we can hardwire the behaviors we want to be able to summon at a moment's notice when the game is on the line. That's the secret of champions — and one of the most important strategies for making good things happen on a daily basis.

MAKE IT HAPPEN PRINCIPLE 12

High achievers take the practice just as seriously as they take the final activity they're practicing for.
"If I had been technically trained, I would have quit."

RULE 13 Accept That Genius Without Ego Is Impossible

That was the curt assessment of King Camp Gillette, founder of the Gillette shaving empire. Gillette was a traveling salesman who decided, in 1895, that there had to be a better way to shave facial hair than holding a knife to your throat — or (even more intimidating) letting a total stranger hold a knife to your throat.

Despite assurances from the "experts" that mass production of the wafer-thin disposable blades he envisioned was impossible, Gillette worked for six long years to perfect the mechanics of the disposable shaving mechanism around which he planned to build an industry. Aided by his partner, William Nickerson, Gillette finally launched his new design in 1903. Sales in that first year were modest to say the least: 51 razors and 168 blades. By the end of the next year, however, the fledgling company had sold 90,000 razors and more than 12 million blades. Each and every one of those slim, disposable blades was designed to be held securely within a protective metal casing. The world of shaving had changed in a way that the experts had insisted was impossible. One man's persistent belief in his own idea had made the difference.

So much for technical training.

Rejecting the advice of "experts" is sometimes necessary, but it's not always popular. In fact, this kind of behavior is often perceived as being just a little bit arrogant. Do you know why that is? It's because this kind of thinking *is* arrogant, and requires a certain level of ego involvement.

To make something really important happen, we must make a conscious effort to *assume* that success is possible for us, even in situations that have stymied other people. To put it another way: *People who get good at making things happen habitually assume that they personally have the right to challenge existing preconceptions.*

The *Random House Dictionary of the English Language* defines genius as "a person possessing an exceptional natural capacity of intellect." I think the key word here is *exceptional*. A genius is nothing more or less than someone who applies logic a little further than others have, someone who is the exception to the rule.

Thinking is really remembering. (We ask ourselves: "How has this worked before?") Logic is thinking applied to a process. (We ask ourselves: "How can I apply what I remember to this situation?") Genius is *exceptional* logic — that is, Gillette's kind of logic, logic *extended* and applied to a particular situation in a new way. (We ask ourselves: "What assumptions can I reject or modify in order to get the result I want?")

You can't get to the third step — the step of genius — without assuming that *you personally* can succeed where others have not.

For my part, I think we all have the chance to be geniuses in at least one area in our lives. To meet the challenge, though, we must acknowledge that genius demands, not simply high scores on some standardized test, but *logic brazenly applied in a new way*. Genius inevitably requires chutzpah, and chutzpah without ego is impossible!

> *Geniuses assume they have the right to make their own surroundings, their own rules, and their own worlds.*

Sometimes I look back on the most fateful decisions in my own life and think: "Boy, did I have a lot of nerve. Who was I to start a business? The experts say that the vast majority of businesses go under within five years! Who was I to put together a training program that claimed to teach people something new about selling? The experts had already said or written everything of consequence about selling, hadn't they? Who was I to sit down and write a book? Weren't the odds against getting a book published long, and weren't the odds against it succeeding in the marketplace astronomical?

Yet, *because* I had a lot of nerve in some key situations, I was willing to apply my own experience and knowledge in new ways. As a result, good things happened to me in all these areas. I launched not just "a business," but a company that grew into one of the largest sales training organizations in the country. I developed not just "a new series of training programs," but a sales *philosophy* that dozens of companies have built their cultures around. I wrote not just one book, but more than a dozen, with over half a million books in print worldwide in a dizzying array of languages.

It all happened because I was willing to let there be an "I" — an ego, a viewpoint — that asked, as King Gillette and countless others had before him, "How can I apply what I know in a way that no one else has yet done?"

That kind of question exemplifies what I call "logic further." It's a fearless, questing, confident brand of logic. It's the purposeful, self-assured appropriation of all the facts at your disposal. It's unapologetic, ego-centered logic. And whether it rattles people's cages or challenges their presuppositions, this kind of arrogant logic must be cultivated if you hope to make the very best things happen in your life on a daily basis.

Too many people get caught in the trap of asking themselves: "What has everyone else done?" Or "What do other people say about this?" Or "What can I do that has the least possible opportunity for error or embarrassment?"

That last question, in particular, is a dagger through the heart of creativity and achievement. Avoid it like the plague. Instead, ask yourself possibility questions. Ask yourself the kinds of questions that Gillette must certainly have asked himself as he built a dynamic new industry from scratch:

- What can I learn from what hasn't worked in the past?

- How can I use the present challenge in a positive way?
- What new approach can I take that others have ignored?
- What can I do that will take me to a level that no one else has yet been to?

For any of these questions to work for you, you must be willing to embrace the word "I" — and not the opinions of other people — as the engine that drives your search for new answers. Genius without ego is impossible!

That doesn't mean you should become self-centered, cruel, or lacking in understanding or compassion toward others. It simply means that you must adopt the mindset that James Joyce captured perfectly when he wrote: "A man of genius makes no mistakes. His errors are volitional and are always the portals of discovery."

MAKE IT HAPPEN PRINCIPLE 13

*Ego is the essential mechanism
driving progress toward any worthwhile goal.*

RULE 14 Become a Virtual Employee

A woman I'll call Millicent applied for a senior marketing position at a major financial services organization. As part of the application process, she prepared an in-depth analysis of the major challenges and opportunities she predicted for one of the company's most important divisions.

Millicent also offered detailed strategies for overcoming each of the problems she saw on the horizon. She took some initiative and built an in-depth strategic plan for the prospective employer. In other words, she assumed that she had already been hired and was personally responsible for executing the duties of the position she wanted.

Millicent used the plan she'd developed as her own notes for answers to the questions she expected during the interview process. As you might expect, she performed pretty well during her interview. As it happened, though, Millicent did not get an offer for the position she was seeking.

What would you do in Millicent's situation? What if you put hours of work into a strategic overview meant to benefit a company you wanted to work for, and then were not offered the job? Most applicants would have done one of two things: either ignore the company and move on to another one (not the best networking approach) or send a nice thank-you letter and check back every couple of weeks to see what has happened recently within the contact organization (a better networking approach).

Millicent didn't do either of those things.

Instead, she asked for a meeting with her contact, who happened to be the president of the company. At that meeting, she handed over the strategic plan she had assembled in preparation for her interview, and said that she hoped the notes would be of use to the company as it launched its new initiative. *Then* she thanked the contact for his time and suggested that the two keep in touch. Again, she acted as though she were already an employee.

The next week, Millicent received a call from the president's office. Would she consider accepting another position at the same level?

This story is a great example of the strategy I call "becoming a virtual employee." It works wonders whether you're hoping to land a job with a top company, trying to capture the attention of a company that would be the perfect market ally for your business, or attempting to land "on the radar screen" of a hot prospect you think would make a great customer for your organization.

> *Right now, you have the power to help people improve what they are currently doing.*

Act like you're already a member of the person's team. Put together a detailed plan that is of immediate and obvious benefit to the contact with whom you're trying to establish a working relationship. If at first you don't succeed, *keep* offering good ideas until you find a way to connect.

One of our salespeople uses a variation of this strategy to break up communications bottlenecks. When he's dealing with a rudderless group, in which nobody in the command structure has any idea who's supposed to make a decision in a given area, our rep takes the opportunity to step into the vacuum and develop an executive summary. The summary is composed for the highest-ranking person in the organization who can take action on his behalf. (Usually, that's the president of the company or the vice president of sales.)

In this executive summary, our rep lays out everything he's learned so far from his discussions with the various contacts in the organizations. He then briefly summarizes his own assessment of the situation and makes a series of action-oriented recommendations. Basically, his plan sounds like this:

> "Over such-and-such a time period, I met with Mr. A, Ms. B, Ms. C, and Ms. D. They told me the following: Fact One, Fact Two, and Fact Three. On the basis of these discussions, my assessment of the situation is that your com-

petitive position would best be enhanced by So On and So Forth, and that you'd be able to measure progress in this area by monitoring Hard Number Areas One, Two, and Three. All this research leads me to make Recommendations A, B, and C. I'll call you next Tuesday at 2:00 p.m. to discuss where we can go from here."

He almost sounds like an employee of the organization, doesn't he? How much more likely is such a summation letter to provoke action than a letter that says, "I enjoyed speaking with you last week and will follow up with Mr. A as you suggested"? It's a hundred times more likely to get the president to actually do something about the recommendation! (Remember, action from the other party is the measurable evidence of something actually happening in any given relationship. It's proof that the relationship is moving forward.)

Use your expertise to perform a little free consulting. Act as though you're working for the other person, even though you're not. If you set up a plan that instantly proves your ability to add value to a given situation, you may even be able to establish yourself as a more important ally than the contact's regular employees. (This is relatively easy to do, because existing employees are usually hesitant to ask questions that will put more work on their plates.)

Ultimately, your goal is not to get a job, or to close a sale, or to secure a formal partnership. All those ideas reflect only one side of the equation — your side. Look at it from the other side, and you'll realize that your real job is to find opportunities to *help the other person do what he or she does a little bit better*. So become a virtual employee. Forward well-thought-out ideas that really are in the other person's best interests. And watch the relationship change for the better.

MAKE IT HAPPEN PRINCIPLE 14

By taking the initiative to develop and forward a detailed plan for your contact's benefit, you can become a virtual employee, and build up essential business alliances with new contacts.

RULE 15 Get Redundant—by Building Backup Plans for Contacts Who Are Depending on You

One of the trainers who works for me shared the following story:

"A couple of months ago, I had to get to the airport, and I arranged for a limo service — I'll call it Low-Rate Limousine — to drive me there. Max Low-Rate, who drives for Low-Rate Limousine, picked me up, and it seemed like Max and I had plenty of time to get to the airport. Unfortunately, there was an accident on the highway. Max and I sat in the car and stared at the traffic jam for 45 minutes. I missed my flight.

"Last week, I used a different limo company to get to the airport. Jack Acme, who drives for Acme Limousine, picked me up. We hit the highway; he saw an accident ahead of us. I saw the accident ahead of us, and I started to worry. Maybe I was going to miss this flight too!

"In a heartbeat, Jack pulled onto the shoulder of the road, took an exit I wasn't familiar with, drove through a series of strange streets I'd never seen before, and then reemerged onto the highway. Suddenly, we were half a mile in *front* of the accident.

"I made my flight! Now, I've lived in this area all my life, and I'd never seen the route Jack used to get me past that accident. I felt pretty lucky to have hooked up with this guy.

"I asked Jack how he managed to find that route. He explained that if one of his passengers is late because of an accident, that passenger doesn't blame the traffic. That passenger blames Jack. So what does Jack do before every trip? He prepares an alternate route — every single solitary time. If something goes wrong, Jack has a backup plan."

> *Deliver what you promised, no matter what.*

Now, here's an interesting question. How often do you think Jack actually gets to use that alternate route?

Who knows? Maybe the answer is one trip out of 20. But when that one time rolls around, he's got a backup plan. And who benefits from that backup plan? The passenger!

Here's another question. Every time one of Jack's passengers is able to get to a flight on time when doing that seems impossible, what happens to that person's loyalty to Jack — and to Acme? More likely than not, Jack wins a permanent customer.

In fact, whenever this alternate-route event actually happens, Jack notices that his customers say the same thing: "Thank goodness I was in your car." Suppose someone has that reaction to Jack's service and then hears about a limo service that offers a ride to the airport for $5 less than Jack charges? Will Jack lose that customer?

Of course not. Jack is probably going to hold on to that business. What does he have to do to make that kind of gratitude happen? Well, 19 out of 20 times, he's got to prepare something that doesn't get used! And 19 out of 20 times, thinking about the customer doesn't put one extra penny in his pocket. But because he always errs on the side of helping the other person — because he always thinks ahead — and goes above and beyond the call — Jack is able to make a dramatic positive impression that twentieth time.

At our company, we always build in backup plans with a contact, because we want a call back from that person. We want our contact to say, "Thank goodness I was in your car!" For instance, a major newspaper wanted us to develop a program to help increase sales in the paper's classified advertisement department. As it happened, the program we actually delivered uncovered some entirely new issues that we hadn't built into our training. Every once in a while, challenges like that crop up in the training business. People start asking questions that nobody anticipated when the proposal and program outline were put together.

Instead of simply leaving those questions unresolved, we called up our contacts at the newspaper and told them that we had a backup plan for just such contingencies: We reserve a trainer and a writer who can work to develop customized material to address the customer's issues at no additional cost. We got them "past the accident" — boosted the department's sales across the board — and won our company a long-term repeat customer!

Always have a backup plan, just in case. If, for some reason, the work doesn't go quite as planned, and you learn that your customer's key goals haven't been fully satisfied, you can instantly put your backup plan into action — and solidify your relationship with a business ally. In my experience, that's the very best way to win the prime spot on a contact's directory!

MAKE IT HAPPEN PRINCIPLE 15

Most of the time you won't need your backup plan to keep your commitments — but every once in a while, you will.

RULE 16 Plan Your Key Questions

One of the motivational speakers I admire most is Charlie Plumb. If you've never seen him in action, you've missed one of our industry's most effective opening moments.

Charlie's audience always enters the auditorium to discover an empty stage. Once everyone is seated, Charlie enters the stage silently and sets up two folding chairs about a yard apart. Then he starts pacing back and forth between the chairs, without a word of explanation, and without even acknowledging the audience's presence.

Back and forth. Back and forth. Back and forth. Any residual chatter or throat clearing in the hall quickly stills, and soon the only noise anyone can hear is that of Charlie walking quietly and intently between the two chairs.

After a few minutes, Charlie stops and explains to the audience that, over a period of six years, he paced back and forth just like that, day after day, in a North Vietnamese prison cell. For six long years, Charlie was a prisoner of war with less than three feet of walking space at his disposal. And that certainly seemed to be everything he had to his name. After all, when the enemy shot him down and dragged him into a tiny cell with nothing more than the rags on his back, Charlie Plumb had absolutely nothing to call his own. Right?

Wrong. At this point, Charlie asks the audience to identify the various internal resources he brought with him into that tiny enclosure. One by one, the members of the audience shout out what Charlie really had at his disposal. Memories. Skills. Courage. Inventiveness. Resilience. Faith.

PLAN YOUR KEY QUESTIONS

Discipline. Time. The ability to think. These and many others were the gifts Charlie Plumb brought into his prison cell.

Plumb's point is that we all have many more resources at our disposal than we give ourselves credit for. The question is: How can we best gain access to them?

Charlie's opening has a way of turning people's minds around in a dramatic and very powerful way. When I heard his story for the first time, I started asking myself: What strengths do *I* have that I'm not exploiting fully? What abilities am *I* not yet using to their fullest capacity? What do *I* always have access to that can empower me when things don't seem to be going well?

I asked myself those questions a great deal over a period of about a week. The answer that came back most consistently was: the ability to plan. What a gift it is to be able to sketch out, in advance, the events I want to undertake once the sun rises! I make a nightly ritual of mentally previewing the day to follow. You can, too.

Any time I feel as though I have "no control" over the events in my life, any time I feel as though I'm "trapped" by a situation, I step back and recall Charlie Plumb's six-year marathon in that miniature cell. Suddenly the various crises of the day just past seem a little more manageable. Suddenly I have a lot of options. Suddenly setting up a to-do list for the next day gets downright enjoyable.

For me, planning the day to come takes many forms. One of my favorite ways to plan is to review my checklist of "foundation questions" about potential customers and business partners. These are basic questions I make a point of asking, questions that will help me get a better idea of what these people do, where they do it, when they do it, how they do it, who they do it with, and whether I can help them do it better. If I'm missing any of this information, I know there's a problem somewhere and I need to dig a little further. Just as Charlie had resources he could always fall back on, I do too: questions!

In my experience, there's always a "next question" I can put on my to-do list to ask new contacts. The three that follow are among the most essential. I recommend that you quietly review your list of contacts nightly and find out which of these questions can help you resume control of your new relationships — and fill "knowledge gaps" in your meetings the following day. Use these questions to make something out of nothing, to identify concerns you can use as assets in the emerging relationship.

Foundation Questions

1. *Whom am I meeting with, and what does that person do?* These are two questions, but they're so closely linked that I take them on at the same time. What's the background of my contact? And how does he or she determine whether a day is a success or a failure? These are vitally important matters for me to discuss with any brand-new contact. Any meeting that doesn't at the very least give me a clear sense of how the other person occupies his or her day is a failure!

    In fact, if I talk to one of my employees about a new contact whom we may be able to help, I always make a point of focusing closely on what our new contact actually *does*. I'm interested not so much in the person's title as in the person's *function*. Let's assume I'm selling phone and data services. The fact that I'm speaking with, say, the telecommunications manager isn't really all that significant. In this setting, telecommunications managers sometimes are the right people — but sometimes they aren't. In many cases, my decision maker could be a controller, an office administrator, or a general manager. Any number of titles may *sound* right, but the only way I can be sure the person is involved in my area of interest is by asking *What do you do?* (See Rule 34 for an innovative strategy for determining who the right contact *is* if you're certain that your present contact *isn't* the right person.)

Who is this person, and what does he or she do? Although these are important initial questions, you never really stop learning about what the other person does.

2. *How does the company make money?* It's surprisingly easy to ignore this issue. Experience has demonstrated to me time and time again, however, that if I don't know how the firm keeps itself afloat, I'm never going be able to help people get any better at anything. How can I be sure that *any* help I offer will be correctly positioned if I don't understand how the organization delivers value to its customers?

There are number of different ways to phrase this question. Some of my favorites are:

"How is it that your company excels?"
"In a market as competitive as yours, how do you attract customers?"
"What kinds of new markets are you exploring?"
"What companies do you see as your major competitors?"

Asking about competitors is particularly important. It not only tells me how the company views itself, but it also points me toward important new leads! Of greater immediate importance, though, is what the answer tells me about how the contact views his or her own company. By focusing on the company's perceived competitors, I can get a sense of the size and complexity of the organization I'm talking to. That means I can effectively tailor my stories, and offer details about similar companies we've been able to help.

How does the company make money? is an important initial question. Still, you never really stop learning about how the company conducts its operations.

3. *What relevant steps have already been taken?* If I'm talking to someone who's trying to get a job with my company, I'll want to know who else is on his or her list of target employers. If I'm talking to a prospect who may be able to use our training services, I'll want to know whether this individual has ever considered working with a sales training company before. If I'm talking to a vendor who wants to work with my organization, I'll try to find out what other companies that firm has worked with in the past. Sometimes you can get this information and sometimes you can't, but it's always in your best interests to ask!

    I always want to find out: "Have you done something like this before? If not, why not? If so, how did you do it last time?" By asking how the person did it last time, I learn about activity patterns. I learn about preferences. I learn about timetables. I learn who was involved the last time around.

    A great way to zero in on this area with a new contact is simply to ask: "If we hadn't gotten together today, what would you be doing instead?" The answers can be extremely revealing. (For more on using this kind of questioning as a powerful conversational opening, see Rule 29.)

What relevant steps have already been taken? is an important initial question. Even so, you never really stop learning about what the contact is doing.

> *Ask the right people the right questions, and you will be successful.*

All these questions are great resources, but it's easy to forget that you have access to them. No matter how challenging the day gets, no matter how many obstacles present themselves, no matter how little influence it may seem that you have over events, you can always resume control of the day to come by reviewing your three "foundation" planning questions for new contacts.

MAKE IT HAPPEN PRINCIPLE 16

Use foundation questions as resources in planning the day to come and building new relationships.

17 Learn to Say, "Next!"

Last month, I was working on a consulting assignment for a Fortune 500 company. My job was to help this company's telephone sales representatives improve their overall efficiency and their sales totals.

Here are the facts I uncovered after a day or so of interviewing salespeople and managers. Put yourself in my shoes. Take a look at the situation I was called in to assess, and ask yourself whether a recommendation leaps out at you. (It should!)

- Managers felt that the phone sales representatives weren't performing up to capacity; quotas were being missed.
- Managers felt that the quotas that had been set were realistic and attainable. (I agreed with them on this point.)
- Representatives were calling contacts repeatedly, until they hit a "brick wall." In other words, if I were the lead, and you were the sales representative, you would probably call me once or twice a week until I told you to stop calling me. Any response other than direct rejection – as in "Leave me alone" or "I won't buy from you" – was considered grounds for another call.
- The typical sale took slightly under four calls to complete.
- After four calls, the likelihood of closing a sale dropped dramatically.

Those are the facts I faced after only a day of talking with managers and representatives. Can you see the solution to the problem these representatives had?

It was really very simple. All the salespeople had to do was *stop making the fifth call*. Statistically, they knew that it would take them four calls to make the sale. On the fourth call, they either closed the sale or they didn't. After four calls, *there was no further point in pursuing a given lead*. Yet there they were calling people, over a period of months, 15, 20, or 30 times just to "check in"! Clearly, this was a major waste of time and effort.

Know when to move on.

I sat the managers and salespeople down and said, "There comes a point in any business relationship when you have to say the magic word: 'Next!' For you, that point is the fifth call. After four calls, I want you to be ready to move on to another opportunity. Over the next 30 days, we're going to conduct an experiment. I want you to call only leads you have contacted three or fewer times, and to use the extra time you win back during the day to contact *brand-new* leads."

A month later, I visited the team. The sales reps had followed my advice — they tracked their calls carefully and made sure never to call any lead more than four times. The results: an across-the-board sales increase of 28 percent!

Before our little experiment, a few of the sales representatives had told me that their philosophy was to keep calling, keep calling, and keep calling some more — until someone actually hung up on them! I think this approach was meant to demonstrate tenacity and goal orientation to the managers. What the salespeople discovered, however, was that their managers were much more impressed with a strategy that allowed them to spend the majority of their time talking to people who were actually interested in talking to them.

The steep sales increase came about thanks to the implementation of a simple rule: *If you have a choice between talking to someone new and talking to someone who has consistently failed to play ball with you, talk to someone new!*

When do you say, "Next!"? When do you decide that it makes sense to move on to another opportunity? When do you evaluate your work and take a close look at the returns you've actually been getting? That's an important question to ask yourself — whether you're working in a sales setting, trying to get something accomplished within your organization, looking for a job, or trying to make anything worthwhile happen. Does it really make sense for you to call the same lead over and over again? Does it really make sense for you to dress up the same ideas that your superiors have shot down 15 times over the past year? Does it really make sense to spend all your free time "checking in" with hiring managers who have said no to you, and no time whatsoever scouting out new employment leads? What else could you be doing with the time you spend on such activities?

To be sure, there is something to be said for persistence. But experience has shown that persistence in the face of a statistical brick wall is not the way to make something happen!

I work one on one with tens of thousands of sales representatives every year. Many of them swear up and down that they "make 100 (or 200, or 300) calls a week." What I inevitably find out is that they are making three or four calls a week to the same 30, 70, or 100 contacts! This is an indefensible waste of time. I think the pattern arises from an insecurity about reaching out to new people. But reaching out to new people is the essential first step to making things happen! (See Rule 24.)

Are you tempted to call a lukewarm (but talkative) lead for the eleventh or twelfth time this month? Are you tempted to spend another hour making a familiar proposal to the same friendly but skeptical colleague at work? Are you tempted to "check in" with someone who won't actually say no to you, but won't move your relationship ahead either? If so, stop and think. How much is that pleasant exchange really going to cost you?

I spent one day gathering information for the telemarketing unit of one of the largest companies in America. I collected a hefty fee for telling people to follow what seemed to me to be a self-evident piece of business advice: *Gauge interest by activity — and don't spend lots of time with people who have demonstrated that they are unlikely to take action on your behalf.* Now you can put that same advice to work in your own career. Don't wait for some consultant to come along and tell you what's obvious!

MAKE IT HAPPEN PRINCIPLE 17

We have a choice:
We can talk to someone who has
consistently failed to play ball with us,
or we can talk to someone new.

RULE 18 — Act Confidently on Good Ideas

As a young man, F. W. Woolworth had a job as a store clerk. At one point, he suggested that his boss promote a "ten-cent sale" to get rid of some excess inventory. The boss indulged his young employee; what did he have to lose? To the boss's surprise, however, the sale was a big success.

This event led the young Woolworth to another idea: Why not open his own store, stocked exclusively with items at the nickel-and-dime price level?

The problem was that Woolworth needed capital to launch such a store. He went to the boss and asked him to supply the funds in exchange for an interest in the new company. The boss was less than enthusiastic; he told Woolworth that the plan was much too risky, and that the idea of stocking an entire store with products at this price level was implausible.

Woolworth felt sure that he was on to something, though, and vowed to find other capital sources. With diligence, he eventually found them. He launched one store quite successfully, and then expanded that store into the chain of "five and ten" outlets that made retailing history. "As far as I can figure out," the tycoon's former boss eventually admitted, "every word I used to turn Woolworth down cost me about a million dollars."

Note three points from that true story:

1. Wooolworth made a specific proposal based on a good idea in order to move a relationship forward.

76

(In this case, the relationship was between himself and his current employer.)

2. Woolworth was *willing to stand behind his own idea*. He assumed responsibility for delivering the results.

3. Woolworth was perfectly willing *to pitch the same idea elsewhere*. He didn't shrivel up and concede defeat after encountering initial resistance from one source. I imagine his attitude during the conversation with his boss could have been summarized as follows: "Here's an opportunity for both of us. If it makes sense to you, I think we can work together profitably. If it doesn't, that's all right too."

> *Don't wait until the end of the day to put your plans in motion. Act now!*

Intelligent, responsible confidence eventually moves the right relationships forward. In my experience, it is a virtually unstoppable force. My favorite definition of this variety of self-assurance is currently making the rounds on the Internet:

> *Confidence*: The appealing ability to act as though you belong exactly where you are, whether that's someone's boardroom or someone's bedroom.

This "appealing ability" has a way of stopping the right people in their tracks. Some years back, I got a cold call from a job applicant. Over the phone, he told me, "I've decided to make a career change and to take my skills and put them to work in the sales training field. You know, I've done a lot of research on your industry. I've looked at the

⌐ out there. And I've decided that, given my ⌐und, I'm going to end up working either for your ⌐ompany or for a company that's a lot like yours. I think we should talk about this. Why don't I come by your office?"

I agreed to the meeting, and eventually ended up hiring him. I wasn't sorry I did, either!

When the moment arises, when the opportunity presents itself, when the opening is clear, *stand behind your idea and use it confidently to try to move the relationship forward.*

Whether or not you succeed in establishing an alliance with the contact in question, you will win! (You'll see what I mean by that under Rule 19.)

MAKE IT HAPPEN PRINCIPLE 18

*Confidence in your own idea
eventually wins allies to your side.*

RULE 19 You Win When You Lose

When I ask you for a Next Step and you tell me why you can't possibly give me one, I win.

Why? Because I get information about exactly what's happening in the relationship, and I'm now free to contact someone else!

A week or so ago, I had a meeting with the vice president of sales at a major Internet company. As that meeting drew toward its close, my contact said, "Listen, this has been fascinating, and you've given us a lot to think about. Let me have a couple of weeks to look everything over, and then give me a call."

Here's my question for you: Is that a Next Step?

Of course not. It's too vague. *After* a couple of weeks — that is, at some undefined point after the two-week period during which most of us schedule our lives — I was supposed to "give him a call." That's nothing. That's no commitment whatsoever. So instead of agreeing to this suggestion, I said, "Why don't we just set up the appointment now?"

Most businesspeople I meet are terrified at the prospect of saying something like that. "You mean, I'm supposed to challenge the contact? He just said he didn't want to talk about it for two weeks! Why on earth would I question that?" The answer: Because your time is too valuable not to! Ask yourself: What's the worst thing that can happen? He'll say no, and he might just tell you why he doesn't want to set up the appointment.

Just as important: What's going to happen if you *don't* try to set up the appointment? You could be strung along for weeks or months!

A statement like "Let me think about it" is basically an attempt to close out the meeting tactfully without passing along much meaningful information. For my part, I want as much information as I can get about *exactly* where I stand with the person as that first meeting closes. So I always make some polite attempt to schedule a Next Step. I have never gotten flak for this, and I usually get much more relevant information about the relationship.

As is my habit, I said, "Mr. Smith, why don't we just set up the appointment now?" And my contact said, "Well, I can't. I'm really busy. Why don't you just call me?" Still no meaningful information. Clearly, there was a problem

79

somewhere, but I didn't have any idea what it was. So I made a final attempt to clarify what was going on. I said, "Mr. Smith, let me ask you a question, just between you and me. Is there something I did wrong?"

The floodgates opened. He started to defend me! "Oh, no, Steve — you haven't done anything wrong! Actually, It has nothing to do with you. The fact is, I really shouldn't have scheduled this meeting at all. I found out last week that my boss has decided to go with somebody else. I meant to call you the other day to cancel, but things just got so hectic that I wasn't able to. We're not going to be able to look at other vendors for another 18 months."

So — I knew it was over. I knew there was no way to move this relationship forward right now. And I was very, very happy!

I was happy because *I now knew exactly what was going on*. I didn't have to spend any time putting together a proposal, or phoning my contact, or trying to determine the likelihood of closure on this sale. The relationship was not moving forward — not today, at any rate — and I could focus my efforts on other contacts. I thanked my contact for his time and for the honesty he showed in explaining where his company stood. I told him I planned to keep in touch next quarter to see how things were going. I shook his hand. And I left.

I won — because I didn't have to invest another six weeks (or two weeks, or one day) following up on a nonexistent lead. But in this case, the only way I could learn what was going on was by giving the other person permission to tell me the truth.

There are many ways for people to say no. The earlier you translate the no, the better.

80

Sometimes people don't want to use the word *no*. They're afraid of hurting our feelings. But if we take the initiative by saying, "Let's set up the appointment now" or "Hey, did I do something wrong?" we are, in essence, *giving the other person permission to tell us what's really happening.* And the more information we have, the better off we are. If there's no point in continuing, our aim is to know that at the *end of the first meeting* — not a month and a half later.

MAKE IT HAPPEN PRINCIPLE 19

*You can give people permission to give you
the straight story by being willing to ask,
"Did I do something wrong?"*

RULE 20 Focus on Your Resources, Not Your Obstacles

Not long ago, a cash-strapped Texas entrepreneur who happened to be a diehard football fan decided to put her season tickets to work for her business. When she went to Sunday afternoon games — a long-standing tradition for her — she began to celebrate her home team's touchdowns and field goals in a creative and visually arresting way. Every time the home team put points on the board, this businesswoman whooped and hollered — and flung about 150 of her company's business cards into the air. The crowd loved it as the white rectangles fluttered down in a gentle white cloud. The cheers always seemed a little louder when people saw the explosion of cards and the gliding rectangles.

Here's the point. After each game, she'd receive three or four calls from high-income prospects (most of them fellow season ticket holders) — people who would otherwise never have heard of her or her company.

When I heard that story, I wanted to know: How did she come up with her brainstorm? I'm not sure what the answer to that question is, but I'm willing to bet that she *didn't* develop her idea by waking up each morning and asking herself questions like these:

- What's going to go wrong next on the PR front?
- Why on earth can't I afford a proper marketing campaign?
- How fair is it that my competitors have a massive radio (television, print, Internet) advertising budget, while I don't?

Instead, I'm willing to wager she asked herself questions like these:

- What do I already have that I can put to better use in order to generate referrals?
- How can I reach out to potentially profitable new business contacts without spending a lot of money?
- What am I doing right now that can put me in touch with new prospects?

Please understand what I'm getting at here. The internal questions we ask ourselves all day long *already* control our point of view and our mental state. Brainstorms (like the business-card celebration) usually come about when we use questions to focus on creative ways to use *what we have* more intelligently. (See Rule 16.) If we use questions to get our brains to focus on what's *lacking*, as opposed to what we've *got*, we tend to find ourselves stuck.

So the point of the business-card story is *not* to get you to buy season tickets in order to get your message out. Instead, I want you to follow this woman's make-it-happen example and ask yourself questions that help you focus on using your existing resources more effectively — in any business situation. When you find yourself tempted to focus on what you *can't* do, make a conscious choice to ask yourself resource-oriented questions. Do this from a relaxed, positive frame of mind, and you'll be amazed at the answers you get in response.

For instance, if you're trying to find the best way to move a certain relationship forward, ask yourself questions like these:

- How can I use my existing resources to develop a better partnership with this person?
- What do I have now that can help make this person's life easier?
- What am I already doing that will help me connect with this person in a more effective way?

These are the questions one of our top salespeople asked himself when he wanted to connect with a huge new company that was considering doing business with our firm. The answer? Call and offer to get together for coffee during the contact's skiing trip. This was an effective use of existing resources, because our sales rep was going to be in the ski resort area anyway, on other business. Since he was already flying halfway across the country, he figured he might as well take a one-hour detour and try to connect with the decision maker one more time.

The result? An in-depth meeting that pointed our salesperson in the right direction — and landed that massive account. *Had he not* scheduled this "leisure" meeting, he would not have gotten the information he needed to close the sale.

Suppose our sales rep had taken a different approach? Suppose he had sat back and asked himself, "Why do decision makers always take vacations at the worst possible time?" We would have lost out!

> *There is always a door somewhere waiting to be opened.*

Consider the following quote from James M. Benham, founder and president of Capital Preservation Fund: "Whenever I have heavy problems, I simply introduce the question to my mind, what the problem is, and, in time, I always get an answer. The answer is always there on time." (From *Creativity in Business* by Michael Ray and Rochelle Myers, Doubleday, 1989.)

Of course, for many of us, it's easier to ask questions that focus on obstacles than it is to ask questions that point us toward efficient use of our resources. Sheer force of habit sometimes conditions us to look at what's missing, rather than what is waiting to be used. That's why we have to make a conscious effort to ask resource-oriented questions, *especially* when cash is tight, deadlines loom, or a relationship is at stake. Remember Theodore Roosevelt's advice: "Do what you can, with what you have, where you are." Emily Dickinson offered a similar insight when she wrote, "Dwell in possibility." That's what people who make things happen before lunch choose to do, over and over again.

MAKE IT HAPPEN PRINCIPLE 20

Dwell in possibility.

RULE 21 Find Your Passion

Everyone agreed that Richard was an unusual high school student.

He seemed to take a deep and abiding joy in subjects that intimidated his classmates. For instance, he relished the challenge of performing in the New York High School Math Meets, and he always seemed to perform superbly in these extremely competitive, high-pressure events. But then, why shouldn't he? At the tender age of 15, Richard had mastered trigonometry and integral and differential calculus. In the following years, he quickly absorbed conics and complex numbers. By the time his senior year rolled around, Richard surprised no one when he won the annual New York University Math Championship.

At just 23 years of age, Richard was recruited to work on the U.S. government's top-secret Manhattan Project, the aim of which was to develop the world's first atomic weapon. This brilliant man would eventually become an eminent physicist; share the Nobel Prize; expand his prodigious intellect and soaring curiosity to such topics as art, linguistics, and music; and, near the end of his days, emerge as a devastating critic of NASA's management and decision-making systems in the wake of the *Challenger* disaster of 1986.

For the genius Richard Feynman, learning was always the guiding passion. Learning, it seems safe to conclude, was his reason for living.

We've all heard the saying: "Nobody ever died wishing he'd spent more time at the office." As popular as that saying is, I think it misses the point. For one thing, I don't believe it's true. I'm sure that there are many people who *do* die wishing that they'd spent more time at the office, because they always had a *blast* at the office. I don't assume there's any reason to think ill of those people, or pity them, or pass judgment on them. I imagine it's entirely possible that Richard Feynman died wishing he could have made one more breakthrough discovery.

Feynman had a mission. We should all have one.

There are millions of people for whom the act of running a company (for example) really is the all-consuming love of their lives. It's what ignites their deepest passions. It's their art, their science, their reason for pressing on. "The office" is why they get up in the morning. It's what they do. By the same token, there are millions of people for whom the act of raising a family is and must be the central focus of life. Again, it's what makes them feel most like themselves. Raising a family is what makes a real difference in the lives of these people. It's the mission they feel, deep down inside, that they were sent to earth to accomplish. There are others for whom growing as an artist over time "means everything." These people become truly animated and energized only when they start talking about their next painting, or poem, or screenplay, or performance.

I believe each of us has an obligation to find a mission, a cause that animates and energizes us and gives us a deep sense of purpose. I believe each of us can identify some task or discipline that we were meant to undertake. I believe every human being can embrace some challenge, some passion, some mission, that fairly shouts out, "This is it. This is worth learning everything you possibly can do in order to do better."

The trick is *finding* that thing. For Feynman, it was the study of advanced mathematics and physics. Perhaps

86

that's not your passion. (It's not mine!) But *something* is your passion. Fortunately, these "mission activities" leave telltale evidence. They're usually profoundly enjoyable for the person who takes on the calling, and they almost always help and energize those who come in contact with that person. Feynman's career is evidence enough. He was one of the few twentieth-century scientists whose writings captured the imagination of a mainstream audience, and his career inspired countless others to expand the boundaries of physics as a field of study.

What do you do well, *and* enjoy doing, *and* do in such a way that it benefits and inspires others? Richard Feynman identified the answer to those questions very early on in his life. Not all of us are so lucky. However, whether you answer these questions at age 7 or at age 97, you *can* answer them. Once you do, you will find what I call a Goal of Self.

Once you decide to focus on this kind of goal and follow through on it purposefully — perhaps for only a few hours a day at first — *it becomes who you are*. This is the kind of goal that transforms what someone else would call "studying math" or "going to work" or "launching a company" or "raising a family" into what *you* call "a mission." This is the kind of goal that's so energizing, so fascinating, so powerful, that it pulls you back again and again. Once you identify this kind of goal clearly, you quickly realize two things: (1) working toward the goal reinforces the best and deepest elements of yourself, and (2) you love doing what you do so much that you cannot get enough of it.

> *What is your Goal of Self?*

My Goal of Self happens to be, "Help businesses, and specifically salespeople, do what they do better." I truly love doing that. I've been doing it for 27 years, and I still stay up late and get up early thinking about ways to do it better. Every time I find some way to move forward on that goal, I want to do it some more. *It's not "a job." It's what I live to do.*

That's my Goal of Self. Someone else's might be to

- Write a truly great play.
- Attain complete financial independence.
- Be a supportive, caring parent.

My experience is that there's usually only one such goal any single individual can focus on at a time. The tragedy is that *most people never even identify a Goal of Self.* Instead, they let others define their goals for them. Let me explain exactly what I mean here. I consider myself successful — and not simply because I run a profitable company. (That's a side benefit.) I'm successful because *I love what I do.* I found something that jazzes me!

The boxer George Foreman was once quoted as follows: "If I see what I want real good in my mind, I don't notice any pain in getting it." Foreman's single-minded focus was the key to his remarkable success in the ring — and his equally extraordinary career as a television and radio spokesman.

Lots of people are great at "setting goals." But are the goals they set the kind that make them *automatically* look past pain and discomfort and challenge? If no aspect of the goal is self-perpetuating, the result is *no action.* Nothing happens before lunch — or after lunch, for that matter.

Agent: What do you want to do with your life? What's important to you?

Client: Well, I want to be a movie star.

Agent: Are you sure about that? That's the number-one goal? That's what really energizes you?

Client: Absolutely. That's what God put me here to do.

Agent: Okay, what steps are you taking to become a movie star?

Client: Well, I haven't done anything yet, but someday, next week, a year from now, once the kids grow up, I'm going to be a movie star. Look, I've set the date, August 14, 2044 — that's when I'm going to get moving on my career in Hollywood.

I don't know about you, but I live in a world where the most important time frame is generally *what's happening within the next two weeks.* (See Rule 5.) *Look at your schedule for the two weeks ahead. If there is nothing on it that supports your goal, the odds are strong that the goal in question is not a Goal of Self.*

A goal that's set far in the future, a goal that never involves action within the next two weeks, a goal you're not willing to take action on *now* and evaluate *now*, is a goal that isn't doing its job. It's not your Goal of Self. It's not self-perpetuating. It doesn't jazz you enough to get you to find some way, any way, to take action and evaluate that action.

Whether you're now able to spend 30 minutes a day or 10 minutes a day on it, there is, at this very moment, a mission waiting for you to claim it. There is something you believe, deep down inside, that you were meant to do in this life. It's something that lights your fire the moment you even think of it, something you enjoy at a fundamental level that benefits or inspires everyone who comes in contact with it.

What is it? Take a moment to identify your mission before you proceed to Part Two of this book. Write it down.

MAKE IT HAPPEN PRINCIPLE 21

You must identify your Goal of Self.

Make Something Happen by . . . Using a Process That Gets You to the Next Step

RULE 22 Rewrite the Rules Whenever You Can

Swifty Lazar had a problem. He couldn't seem to interest a single Hollywood movie studio in a major novel that one of his clients had written. It seemed that he'd knocked on every door, talked to every studio contact, and pitched every angle — and no one was signing on.

Maybe the problem was the sweeping story line. Could it all fit in two and a half hours? Maybe the difficulty was the money Lazar was asking for. Or perhaps his contacts were simply reluctant to attach themselves to the genre his author had selected, an epic family drama. Whatever the obstacle was, the stark fact remained that there was no buyer. Yet.

Instead of throwing in the towel, Lazar started asking a simple question about his situation, a question that all high achievers pose habitually for themselves. My guess is that his question sounded like this: "How can I use what I already know to rewrite the rules of the game I'm playing?"

A question like that can lead to a whole new sequence of powerful questions: "What else have I sold that could help me make progress on my goal? What different strategies can I use to 'package' what I have to offer? What other formats, what other media, what other audiences can I exploit? How else can I use what I have and what I know to benefit one of my potential allies?"

Eventually, the answer came: television. Lazar could turn the novel into a television show. Not a full-scale television *series*, mind you, but a relatively short sequence of episodes that told the novel's massive story. A network

93

television *event*, one with a beginning, a middle, and an end, to be aired over a period of evenings. A "miniseries."

No one had ever turned a novel into a short dramatic television series for American commercial television before. But who was to say such a thing couldn't be done?

As it turned out, it *could* be done. The novel was Irwin Shaw's *Rich Man, Poor Man*. The resulting production was a huge critical and commercial success — and a landmark in the history of American television. Lazar's masterstroke not only opened up untold opportunity for his client, for the ABC television network, and for himself; it also charted a path for future blockbuster miniseries programs. It's fair to say that without *Rich Man, Poor Man*, there would never have been such network achievements as *Roots* and *The Thorn Birds*.

And it all came about from one man's willingness to rewrite the rules.

What did Lazar actually do? He found a new way to implement his product, a new application for what he had to offer. He *reshaped* the property and, in so doing, found a way to help people do what they were already doing a little bit better. (Okay, a *lot* better. The ratings for *Rich Man, Poor Man* were extraordinary.)

So — how can you rewrite the rules? What can you reshape in your business? Making big things happen is often a matter of understanding the concept of "product malleability." Product (or service) malleability simply means *using your resources, experience, and insight to adapt what you already offer to new situations*. This is one of those business skills you really can't afford to ignore.

It's amazing how product malleability can instantly transform the message you send to a potential business ally. Let me give you an example of what I mean. Back before everyone had a mobile phone, my organization was asked to monitor the calling habits of telephone sales representatives at one of the nation's largest long-distance companies. These representatives were supposed to establish new relationships with small business owners. As I listened to the calls, I noticed that the prospects often grew indifferent or harsh when the reps suggested, "We can save you money" or "We can show you how to grow your business."

The unspoken message from the salesperson was: "We're a big company; we know more about your business than you do." That message wasn't helping the cause. I trained the reps to take a different approach. Once they had a conversation going, they began to offer a story like this: "Mr. Recording Studio Owner, we were recently able to help someone in your industry, the music industry, use our prepaid phone cards to improve relations with key clients. These were people who were using the recording facilities on short notice. When our client gave his customers these cards, they were able to keep in touch with him much more easily from anywhere in the country, their other calls were easier to handle, and the relationship with the studio owner improved. He booked a lot of long-term business from those customers. It's interesting; a lot of people think of those cards simply as a convenience for their employees. Actually, they can really improve your bottom line by helping you retain customers."

That's product malleability. The reps we trained to develop these kinds of stories had much better conversations with their prospects, and they showed a measurable improvement in their sales totals.

What new combination of services or new product application can you find? What new way can people use or apply what you offer to get where they want to go more quickly, efficiently, or profitably?

All truly great entrepreneurs, salespeople, and business leaders have enhanced skills when it comes to product malleability. They know how to bend and shape their products and services so that they have more than one option in any given situation. They're excellent at matching what they offer with what people want to do. They're experts at stepping back and asking, as Lazar obviously did, "How could this product be repositioned in a new way that benefits everyone?"

The best way to improve your product malleability skills is to develop a *deep* knowledge of exactly how what you offer has been used in the past — and why it was used that way. Once you know that, you're better prepared for new situations. In fact, one of my main goals in any business setting is to be able to supply lots of stories of the various ways that different companies have used my services to grow their businesses. I strongly suggest you prepare at least 10 such true stories.

> *Know 10 stories that show how you have helped 10 other people or organizations.*

My goal in developing such stories is simple. I want to be able to pass along examples of how people have worked with our organization *and* why they chose to work with us in that way. By focusing on both how and why, I find I'm in a better position to adapt what I offer to new contacts. I can offer stories of how and why customers have bought from us in the past, and that means I have the chance to add value to the new people I am speaking with. The more ways I can think of to highlight a potential benefit, the more likely people are to play ball by sitting down to meet with me.

When you get right down to it, the biggest benefit you can offer is your own experience and insight — your ability to apply what you do to a number of unique business settings. Although you don't know more about a new contact's business than that person knows, you do know how such businesses are growing by using your services and services like yours. You're the expert at identifying the many things you do — and can do — to add value to other people's operations!

Follow Lazar's example. Think creatively to help other people visualize how a new approach could work. Use your own past experiences to develop new applications for what you have to offer. Rewrite the rules — and make something happen.

MAKE IT HAPPEN PRINCIPLE 22

*You should be prepared to share 10 true stories
that illustrate how you can use what you have and
what you know to benefit others.*

RULE 23 Put the Times Square Principle to Work for You

Right now, there's a man standing in Times Square in New York City who has mastered one of the essential principles for success in business.

Before I tell you about him, though, let me ask you a question about Times Square itself. If I were to stand on 42nd Street and Broadway and simply stick my hand out during rush hour, do you think anyone would ever put any money into my hand?

When I ask this question in seminars, there's usually a pause before someone in the group says, "Sure. Eventually, someone would probably give you some money." And that's the right answer. With all the people passing by, eventually I would catch somebody's eye, and that person would stop and put a quarter or a dollar or maybe even more into my hand. It might take a while, of course, but it would happen.

What would happen if I used a cup instead of simply holding my hand out? Would I get the same amount of money, or slightly more? If you had to bet $100 on the correct answer to this question, which side would you bet on? I know how I'd bet. I'd bet that I'd pull in somewhat more money by holding a cup than I would by just sticking my hand out.

Well, what if I had a cup and a bell? Would I make more money than I would if all I did was use a cup? It stands to reason, doesn't it?

And suppose I had a cup and a bell and a sign that read "Please help me"? Do you think I'd do even better than before? Sure I would.

Now suppose I used the cup, the bell, and the sign that read "Please help me" — *and* started looking people in the eye and saying, "Can you help me get home tonight?" Would I get even more money?

Of course I would. Why? Because I'm enhancing my pitch.

At this very moment, there is a gentleman standing in Times Square who sells plain business-card cases. He holds one of the cases up and says, "Wanna buy? Wanna buy? Wanna buy? Wanna buy? Wanna buy?" He keeps that up for hours. He stands there all day. And at the end of the day, his chauffered limousine comes to pick him up and take him home.

What has he figured out?

Clearly, he's got an understanding of the numbers involved. He knows that thousands upon thousands of people pass him by every day on their way to work. Some 42 million people pass through 42nd Street and Broadway every year!

The man knows his numbers. He doesn't expect to sell 42 million business -card cases every year. He doesn't lose sight of his goal when someone walks past without buying a business-card case. He sells only to a small percentage of the people he sees. But he does very well for himself.

This is the reality of making something happen on a daily basis. This is the Times Square Principle: *The more people you see, the better your chances of securing a commitment.* What's more, the better the job you do of enhancing your pitch, the more successful you will be.

Don't make excuses. Make appointments.

Making good things happen on a daily basis is not a question of good luck or bad luck. There are tools and enhancements you can use to strengthen the process of building relationships with the right people. If you use those tools to get your message out effectively to enough people, you win! If, on the other hand, you don't have any effective strategy for getting in front of people, you lose!

MAKE IT HAPPEN PRINCIPLE 23

The more people who know what you do,
the more successful you'll be.

RULE 24 Make Calls for an Hour a Day

Making telephone calls to reach out to new business contacts is pretty close to a religious ritual for me. True story: This morning, I made cold calls for an hour. Even though my company's having a great year. Even though I have lots of salespeople working for me now. Even though we've got plenty of new business booked for months to come.

There's no other way for me to operate. At this stage of my life, I can't not make the calls.

In fact, every single day that I am not in front of a group, I pick up the phone 15 times to call 15 people I have not met with before. I end up speaking to seven of those people, and for every seven people I speak to I will actually set up one appointment. I do that five days a week, which means that at the end of the week I have five new appointments — five new people I have not met with before.

In the real world, all that activity is going to translate into eight appointments per week, not five. Why? Well, think about it. I will see five brand-new people, but I will go back to two or three of those meetings for second and subsequent appointments, all of which means I am averaging about eight appointments a week. My closing ratio is one out of eight. For every eight appointments I go on, I will actually produce one sale, which means I will end up bringing in about 50 new pieces of business each and every year.

Now, why is any of that relevant? Because making something happen is not a numbers game. It's a matter of understanding your ratios, of knowing how many new opportunities are in the hopper and what's likely to happen to them.

Ratios are powerful things. For instance, if I wanted to increase my own income, there are five ways I could do that. The first is the most obvious: I could simply double my number of total calls. That's not the only ratio that's under my control, though. Suppose that, instead of calling 15 people and getting through to seven, I called 15 people and spoke to eight. That would substantially increase the number of people I spoke to over the course of the year.

Suppose I didn't want to worry about that. I could focus my efforts on improving the discussions-to-appointments ratio. In my case, I am averaging one new appointment a day. If I got two appointments a day, what kind of impact would that have? Dramatic!

And suppose that, instead of closing a sale on every eighth appointment, I increased my skills and closed one out of six meetings. As long as I saw the same number of people over the course of the year, I would increase my income substantially.

Finally, I could simply raise the amount of money I get per account. Theoretically, in my case, I could double my fee — but that's not all that realistic. So how can I get more money from an existing account or from a new account? Well, I can sell more services. I can actually penetrate that account more effectively and increase the value of the account. Whatever I decide to do, however, it's going to be in accordance with my understanding of my own ratios. Everything works together; everything I do affects something else in the process. And it all starts when I pick up the phone in the morning!

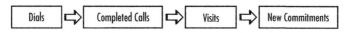

Can you see how the calls drive the whole process?

If we really examine it, we start to realize that our real objective in making sales calls, day in and day out, is simply to get people to use what we have to offer. That's what it is all about. And here's what I want you to remember from this chapter: *We can't get people to use what we have to offer if we don't reach out to them in the first place.*

That means we have to pick up the phone, for an hour a day, regardless of how well or how poorly we think we're doing, and start new relationships with new contacts. When people tell me they have trouble making calls like this on a daily basis, my message to them is short and sweet: *Get over that trouble!* Build up the habit of making calls to new contacts for one hour a day. Build new relationships. Set new Next Steps with people you haven't talked to before.

Success is an appointment you keep with yourself for one hour every morning. I mean that literally. In order to succeed, you have got to take pen in hand to write "make calls to new contacts" into your schedule. That way you'll respect the commitment, and you'll be much more likely to honor it. If you were to look at my daily planner, you'd see that the time from 7:30 to 8:30 in the morning is spoken for on the days when I'm in my New York office. (By the way, that period is a great time for reaching people before their day has started to attack them; you can connect with a lot of early risers if you start making calls at 7:30.) It is essential that you actually block out the time by writing it into your daily planner. So do that!

Whether or not you sell for a living, you want to make new commitments happen. If you don't, then you're wasting your time reading this book!

> *The best, simplest, and most reliable way to ensure that new commitments happen on a regular basis is to devote an hour a day to phone calls that initiate contacts with new people.*

So what exactly do you say on the phone? How do you make the calls? What happens when people interrupt you? You'll learn the answers to those questions later in the book. For now, understand that a daily commitment to one hour of telephone contact with new people is a *mandatory* step for making good things happen in your business, your career, and your organization.

MAKE IT HAPPEN PRINCIPLE 24

Whether you sell or not, commit to an hour a day of reaching out to new people on the telephone — and schedule this hour in your daily planner.

RULE 25 Know the Buy-in Process

I know of two actors; each was looking for voiceover work in industrials. (Those are video and audiotape productions meant to be used as training materials in a business setting.) Each actor took a different approach in getting this kind of work.

One actor met with every company she could track down that was involved in any kind of video or audio training. Her typical conversation sounded like this: "I've done 16 different kinds of audio work in the past; I've also got extensive stage experience. I've worked with Directors A, B, C, and D. My educational background is with This, That, and the Other training program, and I'm deeply trained in Such and Such acting technique."

The other actor met with the same kinds of decision makers, began the meeting by introducing herself in a sentence or two, and then started asking questions. What kinds of training films and audiotapes did the company specialize in? Who were its primary customers? Why did the company focus on that segment of the market?

Can you guess which person got more work? You've got it — the one who put the focus on the other person during the meetings.

That story illustrates a key success principle, one that virtually every outstanding salesperson eventually picks up. People who walk in the door talking about how perfect their "solution" is instantly get shot down or (worse) ignored forever once the meeting concludes. Then there are people who go in, meet with the prospect, and ask, "I'm just curious: What do you do here? How do you do it? Where do you do it? Who do you do it with? Why have you chosen to do it that way?" These salespeople get a different response, the kind that allows them to put together a solid plan that will ultimately lead to the use of their product or service. I've seen this happen time and time again. Now, I don't mean to say that the first group of salespeople *never* close a sale. But I am suggesting that they are far less successful than the second group of salespeople.

Now here's the fateful question. *Why* does the second approach work better than the first approach?

My answer: It works because getting someone to buy into your idea is more a matter of finding out *what makes sense* to that person.

Under Rule 26, we'll look at the actual words you need to say to initiate brand-new relationships with contacts during your daily calling hour. Before we do that, though, I want you to step back and look at another question, one that will help you understand why you're making those calls in the first place.

What is effective selling?

Remember, all of us are engaged in selling ideas, all the time, though not all of us sell our ideas at the highest level of effectiveness! Just about all of us can recall a situation in which someone tried much too hard to "sell us" on something that seemed to have little or no relevance to what we were doing. So — is effective selling the same as convincing? Is it the same as developing a "watertight" logical argument? Is it the same as reciting your credentials at length to someone who would rather be somewhere else?

Obviously not. I think the best definition of effective selling — of ideas, training programs, business alliances, or anything else — has to do with learning *what other people do*. By that I mean learning

What they DO.

How they DO it.

When they DO it.

Where they DO it.

Who they DO it with.

Why they DO it that way.

And then

Helping people DO it better.

> *You can't sell your idea to someone if you don't*
> *understand how the idea will help that person do*
> *what he or she does better.*

When salespeople ask me how to close a sale (and they often do), I tell them that the best way to do it is simply to come back to the prospect and say, "Ms. Prospect, this really makes sense to me. What do you think?" That really is an incredibly effective closing technique. In my view, it's the very best one out there! Once you ask that question, the prospect has to respond to what you've said; you've thrown out the ball. But — and here's the catch — what you've proposed will make sense to the prospect only if it matches perfectly with what the prospect is doing. And the only way your plan can do *that* is if you truly understand what the other person's business is, how it functions, and why it's been set up in the way that it has. That means you must ask what the other person does!

Suppose you walked in to meet with a new contact and noticed a large brown cow behind the desk next to the prospect. How would you react? My guess is that you would say something like this: "Gee, excuse me, but why is that brown cow sitting next to you behind the desk?" As natural as that question is, though, most of us have grown accustomed to ignoring the obvious. We're too eager to talk about our stage experience (or anything else we've memorized) to say, "I'm just curious. Why do you have what you have right now?"

Making things happen means becoming a messenger of change. And before we can change anything, we have to know what's happening right now. We have to know what possessed that contact of ours to bring a big brown cow into the office! After all, whatever the reason was, we can rest assured that *it made sense to the person at the time!* Otherwise, why would a cow be next to the desk?

Let me reiterate: To win buy-in for our ideas, we have to come up with a suggestion that *makes sense* to the other person. But we can't expect to make that kind of suggestion unless we know a great deal about what our contact is doing. So how do we learn that?

Take a look at these boxes.

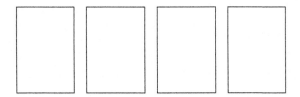

The boxes represent the four steps of the buy-in process. In other words, this is the process that begins right after you and the contact connect for the very first time. Now, during my training programs, I always ask salespeople to tell me what they think the objective of the very first step — the box on the far left — is. Typically, they tell me the objective is to create rapport, or to meet the contact, or to get in the door. Interestingly enough, though, the *real* objective of the first step is simply to get to the second step.

That means that when you are visiting with someone for the first time, or on the telephone with a person you've never spoken to before, what you are trying to do, first and foremost, is *move the process forward*. The objective of the first step is to get to the second step. The objective of the second step is to get to the third step. The objective of the third step is to get to the fourth step, which is commitment, or buy-in.

That's the step we looked at a moment ago. It's the step where, after you say, "Gee, you know what? This makes sense to me. What do you think?" The other person says, "Yeah, you're right. It does make sense. Let's get started." Now, you'll recall that the key to getting that kind of answer is putting together the proper plan or proposal. What's that proposal going to be based on? Information about what the other person does! How are you going to get that information? You're going to ask for it. And when are you going to start asking for it? Right after your opening, which typically is your first contact with the person.

The Buy-in Process

Here's what the buy-in process looks like when it's laid out in detail. The four-step model describes the shifts related to *any* idea that *anyone* sells to *anyone* else. Most businesspeople are familiar with this progression on an intuitive level, but they aren't consciously aware of where they are in the process at any given moment. As a result, they don't know when they're in a position to move from one step to the next, and they are rarely in a position to ask directly for the appropriate Next Step.

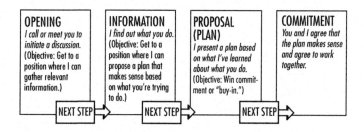

A few side notes are in order. First, these boxes should *not* be taken to suggest that you must spend equal amounts of time in each step. As you'll learn under Rule 35, most of your time with any given contact should be invested in the information-gathering step. Second, even though I haven't listed an objective for the fourth step, there is usually some new project or initiative on the horizon that will help you expand the relationship. In most cases, the objective of the fourth step, the commitment step, is to execute the plan so well that you can start all over again and begin talking about a new area where you can add value to what the person does.

Please take a moment to review the four steps in the diagram above. Most of the rules in Part Two will depend on your familiarity with these principles.

In theory, the progression is deceptively simple-looking: *Opening (leads to) Information (leads to) Proposal (leads to) Commitment.* In practice, however, you'll find that a little experience and analysis are necessary before you can develop a sense of which of these steps you're in at any given moment with any given contact. Before long, however, you will find that evaluating your relationships in this way becomes second nature.

In order to make something happen, you must be willing to focus, not on how wonderful you are or your idea is, but on *where you are in the process — and how you can best move the relationship with the other person forward.* The director Rob Reiner once told one of his actors, "This scene is not about you; it's about the other person." That was good acting advice — and great advice for moving business relationships forward too.

To win buy-in for our ideas, we have to be able to make a suggestion that makes sense to the other person. But we can't expect to make that kind of suggestion unless we know a great deal about what our contact is doing. For that to happen, we must understand exactly where we are in the buy-in process — Opening, Information, Proposal, or Commitment — and understand that the purpose of every step is really to move forward to the following step.

MAKE IT HAPPEN PRINCIPLE 25

You must understand what the other person is doing if your plan is to make sense.

RULE 26 Get It All Down in Black and White

Shelly shrugged her shoulders and raised her palms as if to say, "What do you want from me? Some things are impossible."

"I tried doing what you said," Shelly explained. "You know, making the calls for an hour a day. The problem was that it sounded completely stilted and fake. After a couple of days I gave up. I guess I'm just the kind of person who can't use a script. After all, scripts really do make you sound canned and unnatural, don't they?"

That's what I heard from Shelly during the follow-up session to one of our training programs. Sometimes salespeople (and entrepreneurs, job seekers, real estate agents, recruiting professionals, and anyone else who has to build new business alliances) can get intimidated by the idea of developing a consistent approach to telephone prospecting. My experience is that, when this happens, the problem generally *isn't* that the person has a constitutional inability to recite certain words in a spontaneous-sounding way. In this case, I *knew* that wasn't the problem. Earlier in the program, I had asked the members of the group to engage in a standard "icebreaker" exercise: Everyone was to share the most unusual event that had ever happened on the job. Shelly had shared a story about a

110

strange customer that left the group in stitches! She had delivered her story with perfect timing, and had been supremely confident and absolutely spontaneous as she did so.

Now, as Shelly looked at me with her "What do you want from me?" expression, I challenged her.

"Don't tell me," I said, "that you've never told that story about the odd customer before. You delivered it like a real pro! It sounded perfectly spontaneous too. I'm going to guess that you've told that story at least 20 times since it happened."

"Oh, sure, I have," Shelly told me. "I've told that story at every party I've gone to for the past five years. But that's not a script. That's just something I said over and over again until it became second nature."

Well, that was a distinction that eluded me. Nevertheless, I continued by trying to explain to Shelly that film actors rely on scripts, and somehow *they* don't sound canned or stilted. I asked her to name her favorite movie. Shelly's favorite film, as it turned out, was *Forrest Gump*.

"Did you ever hear," I asked, "about how Tom Hanks prepared for that role?"

"No," she said.

"He sat down with a friend and read the entire screenplay, camera instructions and all, right out loud. Not once. Not twice. Not three times. But *dozens* of times. He kept reading it over and over until it became second nature. It was kind of like that story of yours. He just did it again and again. And if you practice your call approach that way, it will become just as comfortable to you as that story is to you now. When you make calls, you'll fall back on the 'script' instantly, without even thinking. It will sound perfectly spontaneous. Will you give it a try?"

She agreed — and the next month, when I checked in with her, she sounded utterly self-confident and completely at ease on the phone. Her total appointments had grown dramatically.

I share Shelly's story with you because I know telephone scripts can take a little getting used to. Still, it is essential to build your own personalized script, and stick with it until you know it by heart. Start with your own words, and then practice so much that you no longer need the physical piece of paper. Internalize the script completely.

Use the ideas presented below to develop a script that suits your own style, and then practice it over and over again until you can recite it instantly upon being awakened from a sound sleep. You will get great results, just as Shelly did, when you make your daily calls. That's a promise.

You're about to learn how to put together a calling script that will help you connect with new people. Understand that the *point of any phone script is to get you interrupted.* You want to get the first negative response out on the table so you can deal with it. (See Rules 8, 27, and 28.)

> *Standardize your initial phone call to new contacts — get so familiar with it that you can recite it in your sleep.*

The Calling Script

First, we'll look at the basic script, and then I'll give you a more advanced version. You can decide for yourself which approach makes the most sense for you. Each uses four elements. If you change the order, omit or alter any elements, or add material that's not in the outline, your performance will suffer.

Element 1: The Attention Statement. The first thing you want to do when you get through to a new lead is to get that person's attention. The best, simplest, and most professional way to do this in a conversation is simply to say "Hello" and then mention the person's name. Some people use the first name ("Joe"), and others prefer the last name ("Mr. Robertson"). Use whatever style you feel comfortable with and whatever you feel is regionally appropriate.

Element 2: The Identification Statement. The next step is to identify yourself and your company, if appropriate, in a little commercial. As long as you keep it brief, you can use just about any words you want. For example: "This is Frank Danvers, from D.E.I. Management Group. I don't know whether you've heard of us, but we're one of the leading sales training companies in the country, and we've trained nearly half a million people."

Element 3: The Reason for the Call. The third part of the script briefly cites a benefit that you (or your company) typically deliver to customers (or other people you work with). Here is one approach: "The reason I'm calling you today specifically is that we've been reaching out to companies in the Boston area to set up appointments and tell them about the success we've had with our programs for increasing sales efficiency."

By the way, I'm a firm believer in letting people develop their own scripts, so I want to encourage you to use phrases that work for you, as long as they fit into the basic four-element outline. There is, however, one mandatory element here: the phrase "The reason I'm calling you today specifically is that . . . ." This is highly effective and should be used verbatim.

You can specify a geographical area ("Boston"), an industry ("real estate companies"), or a specific company that the contact has heard of. If you want, you can close out this step with an optional qualifying sentence: "I'm sure that you, like a lot of our customers, are interested in improving sales performance." Your aim is to get some kind of response, positive or negative, to this statement.

Element 4: The Appointment Closing Statement. This final element is focused *not* on selling your product or service, but on selling the appointment. Why? Because you're still in the Opening step, the first box. *You are not in a position to make a recommendation yet.* Instead, you're going to ask for a Next Step by suggesting a face-to-face meeting in a very straightforward way. Here's what it might sound like: "What I'd like to do is set up an appointment to tell you about some of the things we've been doing. Would next Tuesday at 3:00 p.m. work for you?"

(*Note*: In some business situations, it is appropriate to ask for something other than a face-to-face meeting. Many people have successfully adapted this script for use in setting up a "phone appointment" — that is, a chance to talk to the person for, say, 20 to 30 minutes at a specific date and time. Although easily canceled or forgotten, and thus not as strong an indication of interest as a face-to-face appointment, the phone meeting does qualify as a Next Step. My preference, however, is always to request an in-person meeting.)

Remember, people respond in kind. You're focusing on *when* the appointment will take place, rather than *whether* it will be convenient to get together. Offer one time and one time only.

Again, be sure to use your own words, not mine, in developing your script. Hit all four elements, but put them in terms that you find comfortable. Here's how the script we've just developed might read in sequence. Review it

114

carefully. Can you identify all four elements without looking back to the list you just read?

> "Hi, Mr. Robertson. This is Frank Danvers, from D.E.I. Management Group. I don't know whether you've heard of us, but we're one of the leading sales training companies in the country, and we've trained over half a million people. The reason I'm calling you today specifically is that we've been reaching out to companies in the Boston area to set up appointments and tell them about the success we've had with our programs for increasing sales efficiency. I'm sure that you, like a lot of our customers, are interested in improving sales performance. What I'd like to do is set up an appointment to tell you about some of the things we've been doing. Would next Tuesday at 3:00 p.m. work for you?"

So — if that's your opening, what happens next? You remember. You're going to get an initial objection or response. Again, you'll learn about how to deal with those under Rules 27 and 28.

Before you move on, however, take a look at a variation on the basic calling script; it's called the Third-Party Referral. Many of the people we train prefer to use this version. It's a little more advanced, because it requires you to name a specific company you've delivered value to in the past. The referral must be a happy customer or business ally whom your contact can call.

Here's what the Third Party Referral sounds like. Note that it, too, follows the four-element outline.

Element 1: The Attention Statement. "Hi, Bill Jones?"

Element 2: The Identification Statement. "This is Janet Cleary calling from Scranton Associates. I don't know if you've heard of us, but we're one of the fastest-growing literary agencies in the country, and we were recently featured in an article in *Publishers Weekly* entitled "Three to Watch: The Most Dynamic Young Agencies in America."

Element 3: The Reason for the Call. "The reason I'm calling you specifically is that we just did a book authored by one of your counterparts, Bill Jessup, who's the president of Jessup Internet Strategies. It's been very successful, and I'm calling a few CEOs at prominent firms in other industries to set up appointments and talk about the possibility of developing new trade book proposals with them."

Element 4: The Appointment Closing Statement. "What I'd like to do is set up an appointment with you to tell you about the project we were able to put together for Bill Jessup. Would next Tuesday at 3:00 p.m. work for you?"

Which of the two approaches do you feel most comfortable with? Pick one and develop a calling script based on it before you proceed further in this book.

I know I've given you a lot to do in here. All the same, it's very important that you take at least 30 minutes to develop and *practice* a script based on one of the two models you've just read. You will be using a version of one of these scripts, couched in your own words, during your daily calling time.

You will need to practice your script *so often that you can recite it instantly, and without hesitation, in any situation*. That's a lot of practice! Typically, it takes one of our program participants three weeks of approximately one hour of practice calls per day to get the script "down cold." You should expect to spend about that long mastering your own script.

MAKE IT HAPPEN PRINCIPLE 26

*Develop a phone script that incorporates an
Attention Statement, an Identification Statement,
a Reason for the Call, and an Appointment Closing
Statement. Use it at least an hour each day to make
calls to new contacts.*

RULE **27** Turn Responses Around

At our company, we're pretty intensely focused on dealing with negative responses in a positive way. As you're about to learn, we view *any* initial response as a reason to give the person we're calling another chance to throw the ball back to us — and thereby become an active prospect. We take (almost) any opportunity to get someone moving through the buy-in process. Our sales trainer Steve Bookbinder told me about one decision maker he called who wouldn't commit to an appointment. "I can't meet with you next Friday at three, Steve," the executive supposedly said. "I have a terminal illness and I only have a week to live." Steve allegedly thought about this for only a moment before saying, "Well, that's no problem. What are you doing tomorrow morning at ten?"

I have a feeling that's not *quite* a true story, but it does illustrate an important point. If an adult throws a large plastic ball at a one-year-old, the one-year-old doesn't catch it. But if an adult throws a large plastic ball at a four-year-old, the child will usually catch it and throw it back.

Just as you learned to anticipate catching and throwing a ball when you were growing up, you can learn to anticipate the things that people say to you on the phone, and you can develop strategies for handling just about anything that comes your way.

Whenever you make a prospecting call, though, the response will come at you very fast. It's more like a 90-mile-per-hour fastball than a big, slow playground ball. Fortunately, you have an advantage. You *know* that the person is going to give you a response. (See Rule 8.) And you're going to be ready when that happens.

All responses can be anticipated.

You may be surprised to learn that there are really only a handful of responses you are likely to hear when you try to win an initial commitment on the phone. Specifically, all the so-called objections break down into one of five categories. (I say "so-called" because the relationship is so young that the person on the other end of the line doesn't really have anything to object to yet.) The trick is to *turn responses around effectively and repeat some variation on your Appointment Closing Statement.* In other words, deal effectively with the response and politely restate your request for a Next Step.

Here are the five response categories.

Response 1: "Not Interested." People can tell you, "Let me stop you right there — I'm just not interested." You've heard that before, right? Actually, there are a lot of different ways to say "I'm not interested." People can say "I have no need," "I have no money," or even "I've had a problem with outfits like yours in the past." Those all fall into the

118

category of "not interested." And your turnaround here is going to be very simple. It's going to focus honestly on what you've done for other people who told you the exact same thing. Your response is going to use that past history to emphasize the benefit of working with you. When you hear any variation on "not interested," you're going to say something like this:

> "You know, many of the people we work with have had that same reaction, until we had a chance to show them how we could benefit them. Let's get together. How's Tuesday at 2:00 p.m.?"

Response 2: "Happy Now." A very popular response to a prospecting call is "We're happy now." Again, people don't always say the words "We're happy with what we've got now." They may say, "Steve, I'm all set," or "We just signed with so-and-so," or "We've got someone who handles this for us already." The response to the different variations on "Happy now" is also going to be simple and effective.That turnaround sounds like this:

> "Actually, a lot of the people we work with told us the same thing, until we had a chance to show them how we could actually complement what they were already doing. Let's get together and talk about it. How's Tuesday at 2:00?"

It's that simple, that direct. By the way, when you're dealing with a "happy now" objection, emphasize how your ideas "complement," "fit into," "enhance," or "match" what the person is already doing.

Response 3: "Mail Me Something." Another very common response sounds like this: "Steve, why don't you just send me some literature?" Remember, your goal is to set up an appointment, not to send literature. You've got a couple of options here. My personal suggestion is simply to say this:

"I prefer not to send literature; I'd really rather get together instead. How's Tuesday at 2:00 p.m.?"

There are a couple of variations here. You can also say:

> "You know, Ms. Jones, I've got a better idea. Why don't we just get together. How's next Tuesday at three?"

> "Couldn't we just get together instead? How's Tuesday at 2:00 p.m.?"

> "Well, I'd be happy to fax over some of our literature, but the reason I'm calling is to set up an appointment. How's Tuesday at three?"

Many people feel they must send literature to contacts they know virtually nothing about. My philosophy is that you're out to win commitments — and commitments, as a rule, are demonstrated by a contact's willingness to schedule time to work with you within a two-week period that starts today. If there's no such willingness, and no other evidence that the person has decided to play ball with you, you've struck out in the first box of the buy-in process. (See Rule 25.) There's nothing wrong with that; it happens all the time. The problem is that so many people hear the words "Just send me some information," and translate them into something like the following: "I absolutely must learn more about your organization." A more accurate translation is probably "Leave me alone." In the vast majority of cases, simply sending literature without scheduling an appointment really gets you absolutely nothing — because there was never any interest in the first place.

Response 4: "No Time." Another objection you're likely to hear is "I don't have time." There are a whole lot of variations on this one: "Steve, I'm on my way out the door to catch a plane to London." "Steve, I've got a meeting in two minutes. I simply can't deal with this right now." "Steve, the College of Cardinals is out in the hallway. They need some advice, and it sounds urgent, so I'm going to have to call you back." The turnaround for this response actually makes the other person's lack of time work in your favor. Here's what the turnaround sounds like:

> "Well, the only reason I was calling was to set up an appointment. Would Tuesday at three work?"

The fifth kind of response is one we'll cover in detail under Rule 28. It's a direct question or extended statement, an attempt by the other person to get you to sell over the phone before you know anything about the person or the organization. That's probably the trickiest of all the responses you're going to come across, but as you'll see, it too can be turned around easily.

All these turnarounds should be practiced so thoroughly that you can deliver them without hesitation or awkwardness. By the way, you'll quickly discover that the second response you hear on the phone often involves a new issue that has little or nothing to do with the first one you heard. Understand that the first response from a contact is a shield. It's there so the person can get back to whatever he or she was doing before you called. You want to try to turn it around and set up the appointment — not argue with the person or get involved in an extended conversation. (In fact, the longer a prospecting call continues, the less likely you are to schedule the appointment.) By simply resuming control of the conversation, and throwing the ball back to the other person by asking for an appoinment, you are making an attempt to move the relationship forward. Something's going to happen. Either you'll win a commitment at the end of the call or you won't. Most of the time you won't. But you'll know where you stand, and you'll know who's playing ball with you.

Once you get past three negative responses, and you don't have a commitment, it's time to move on to another call. Don't get into any debates. The aim is simply to win a commitment. Remember my daily numbers: 15 calls, seven discussions, one appointment. You may want to use those numbers as target figures until you establish working ratios of your own.

The principles you've just read, combined with the script models you used under Rule 26, are the foundation tools you need to reach out to new contacts. Once you master these ideas, and the technique discussed under Rule 28, you'll be ready to handle the most common negative responses that come your way during your morning calls.

MAKE IT HAPPEN PRINCIPLE 27

There are simple turnarounds to the most common phone responses.

RULE 28 Don't Get Sidetracked— Use the Ledge

In the 1988 presidential campaign, Vice President George Bush gave his opponent Michael Dukakis a lesson in "staying on message."

During that campaign, Bush lambasted his opponent's liberal politics over and over again. Dukakis, the Massachusetts governor, was trying valiantly to position himself as a moderate and attract middle-of-the-road voters. Somehow, though, Bush dominated the news cycles with inventive visuals and startling sound bites that always seemed to incorporate the "L word." Whether the issue was prison furloughs, the Pledge of Allegiance, or tax policy, Bush always seemed to find a way to redirect the discussion to the subject of his opponent's liberal bias.

It worked. Bush kept returning to his core message. Dukakis had no comparable core message that resonated as powerfully with the public. Bush won.

The lesson? People who learn how to *stay on message* are more likely to make things happen than people who get sidetracked. What is the ultimate tool for staying on message in a business conversation? I call it the Ledge. A ledge is where we go for a foothold when there's nowhere else to turn. It's also the single most powerful conversational tool (and conversion tool!) you have on the phone.

As you'll learn, the Ledge is very easy to adapt to the fifth category of response, which is probably the toughest category: direct questions and extended statements from the contact. These kinds of responses are difficult to handle because they usually don't sound like negative responses at all. A question like "How much do you charge?" is often impossible to answer before you know what the other person is doing. Similarly, a long conversation may be designed to remove you from consideration without the relationship-building and information-gathering step of a face-to-face meeting. The Ledge lets you deal effectively with both kinds of responses, and steer the conversation back to your request for a Next Step.

In addition, the Ledge can be used to turn around virtually any response you hear during a phone conversation in which you're trying to obtain a Next Step. If you practice it regularly, you'll become an expert at "staying on message," and will find ways to adapt the technique to all kinds of discussions.

Let's assume that the person you're talking to asks you a direct question — one that has nothing whatsoever to

do with what you were just talking about. First and foremost, you are going to anticipate that interruption and
have a short answer ready. So if the other person says,
"What makes your company different?"or "How much do
you charge?" you are going to have a short response prepared. Not the ultimate answer, and not an evasive answer,
but a very brief and truthful answer. After all, if you don't
answer your contact's questions, he or she will not answer
your questions. People respond in kind!

So — you're trying to set up a first appointment, and
you're interrupted with a direct question. The question
you want to get back to is "Can we get together next Tuesday at three?" But you can't simply ask that right away,
because *you've* just been asked a question. That's the bad
news. The good news is that once you *do* answer the other
person's question briefly, you will be entitled to ask a question of your own.

You'll need to position that question midway between
the other person's "How much do you charge?" and the
question *you* want to get to, which is "Can we get together
next Tuesday at three?" You are going to ask something
about what the contact is doing now, something you feel
you could ultimately help the other person to do better.
You're going to use the foothold you get as a result — the
response you receive to that question — as a way to return
to your "core message," your request for an appointment.

Here's what the Ledge sounds like in action:

Prospect: Steve, what makes your company different
from the other companies?

Me: (Short answer) Well, the main thing that makes us
different is that our trainers are also salespeople — so
they have to practice what they preach. (*Without pausing,* I continue by asking) Can I ask you, what are you
doing now for sales training? (That's my "midpoint"
question; it's positioned halfway between what the per-

son just asked me and what I want to return the conversation to, which is the appointment.)

Prospect: Well, right now, we're doing all the training internally. (Now I've got a foothold! Watch what I do with it.)

Me: Is that right? You know, that's really why we ought to set up a meeting. A lot of our clients said that initially, until they found out how what we offered could complement what they were already doing internally. I'd love to get together. How's Tuesday at three?"

> *Use the Ledge to reclaim control of the conversation.*

Did you see it? I resumed control of the conversation. I stayed on message! *Whatever* the person answers in response to my "midpoint" question becomes the reason we *should* get together for a meeting. Suddenly the subject isn't what makes me different from my competitors, but *whether or not we can meet Tuesday at three.*

The Ledge is an extremely powerful communications tool. If I'm asked about price, I can offer any number of variations on my basic answer, all of them accurate and all of them *brief*:

"Well, it costs between this amount and that amount."

"It costs between this range and that range."

"It costs between this percentage of your budget and that percentage of your budget."

Once I briefly and honestly answer that question, as long as I don't hesitate, I can *instantly* resume control of the conversation. Look at it again:

"Well, for a company in your industry, our costs typically range between A and B. (*Without pausing*, I continue by

125

asking) Can I ask you what you're doing now to clean your widgets?"

Once the other person responds, I've got my foothold! Again: *Whatever answer comes back, that's the reason I give for asking for the Next Step.*

> "You know what? A lot of people we work with didn't have any formal widget-cleaning system in place before they saw the benefit of working with us. I'd love to get together with you to talk about this. How's Tuesday at 2:00 p.m.?"

So let's review. You respond *briefly* to the question or statement. You pose a question of your own, which you now have every right to do. ("Can I ask you what you are doing right now to grow your business?" "I'm curious — what are you doing now to reach out to new customers?" "What are you doing now to stay close to your existing customers?" "What are you doing now to service your accounts better?") Then *whatever answer comes back*, you use that as the reason to sit down for a meeting with the person.

Try it! Use the Ledge. Practice it. Stay on message. And get the commitment.

Once you do, start scheduling face-to-face meetings with your contact — and you will if you implement the ideas you've just read under Rules 25 to 27. You'll also want to develop a strategy for moving through the buy-in process with that person. That's what the next few rules are all about.

MAKE IT HAPPEN PRINCIPLE 28

The Ledge is the most effective tool there is for resuming control of the conversation and making something happen over the phone. Practice it until it's second nature, and use it to stay on message.

RULE 29

Ask Why They're Not Working with You Now

Jim, a young salesperson for a major telecommunications company, visited me in New York City. Jim knew very little about my company or the industry in which it operated. He had not been on all that many sales calls in his short career. Uncertain how to conduct the meeting, Jim decided to "improvise" his way through the first few minutes of the discussion.

After a few opening pleasantries, Jim took out a brochure and talked about his own product — we'll call it the ABC brand cellular phone. He talked about how long he'd been selling for his company. He discussed the service arrangements his company offered. In short, he talked about everything *except* what my company did and how cellular phones might be able to help me do that better.

After about five minutes, I started to move around in my chair uneasily. Jim sensed that there was a problem.

"Is there anything I haven't covered?" Jim asked.

"Yes," I said. "You haven't asked me anything about my company. As it happens, we've got a long-term contract for our cellular phone service that I just signed three days ago. I'm locked in with them for the next six months."

Of course, Jim was disappointed at this outcome. He shook my hand, thanked me for my time, and started to pack up his materials. But I insisted that he stick around for a few minutes more.

"Do you have any more appointments today?" I asked.

"Yes," Jim said. "I'm meeting with a big manufacturer later this morning."

127

"What's your opening?"

Jim wasn't quite sure how to respond to this. He asked what I meant.

"When you walked in here," I explained, "you had no idea what you wanted to talk to me about — no idea what information you wanted to get from me. That's not a great way to run a meeting. When you go on your next appointment today, I want you to do me a favor. Start out by asking the person, 'I'm just curious — why aren't you using ABC brand mobile phones?' That will get your meeting off to a good start, because you'll know exactly where you stand with the prospect. You'll also give the other person a reason to start talking about his or her own company. Will you use that as your opening — and then call me and let me know what happened?"

Jim certainly hadn't expected to receive this kind of unsolicited advice, but he agreed to give the technique a try. Later that morning, he walked into another office in another building, shook hands with another prospect, exchanged a few pleasantries, and asked the new question he'd been given. "Ms. Lopez," he said, "I was just wondering about something. I've checked my records and I can tell that you're not using ABC mobile telephones. Why is that?"

The floodgates opened! Jim's new contact explained that each of her sales reps had separate mobile phone accounts with different companies. Six different people were filing six different expense reports every month. There were six different kinds of bills to decipher, and it took a lot of work to straighten everything out.

Jim walked out of that meeting with an order for two mobile phones — and a request to put together a proposal for fifty-five more units the following month. He called me — his unlikely "adviser" — to pass along the good news and to thank me for the help. I'm willing to bet that Jim will never walk into a sales meeting without a prepared opening question again.

Know your first question.

What question will *you* use to begin your meeting with a new contact? Is it based on what the person is now doing? Does it tell you what the person would have done if you hadn't called? Does it tell you why or how the current program is in place?

Here are five points to bear in mind about your meetings with new contacts:

- Those who prepare an opening question have a significant competitive advantage over those who don't.
- The question you ask should be both simple and far-reaching. "Why aren't you working with us?" is an excellent opening question that will let you know *exactly* where you stand with a prospect. So is "Have you ever worked with someone like us before?"
- A good opening question to ask a *former* customer who hasn't given you business in a while is this: "How come we haven't been working together lately?" After all, if there was a product or service problem, you're better off finding out where you stand early in the meeting.
- Once you've used an opening question to get the discussion started, carefully consider each point the other person raises. Follow each one through to its natural conclusion. Don't simply nod and move on to the next topic on your own list.
- Follow up with questions that begin with *how* and *why*. These are the kinds of questions that usually

point you toward the most important information. (See Rules 34 and 35 for more advice on effective questioning.)

MAKE IT HAPPEN PRINCIPLE 29

Know the first question you plan to ask. Find out why the person isn't working with you already.

RULE 30 Live Off Peak

As chief national correspondent and anchor of John King USA, King makes about 100 telephone calls a day to Washington, D.C.'s movers and shakers. His calls, according to the April 1999 issue of *Brill's Content*, are often brisk and to the point: "Hey, this is King — anything going on?"

What's fascinating about King's work philosophy, however, is not *how many* calls he makes but *when* he makes some of his most effective contacts. Among his "tricks of the trade" is a technique for getting people to open up at the end of a long day and share what they know. King learns as many of his sources' car phone numbers as he possibly can. He then calls them during the evening rush hour, when there's nothing much to do. Nothing much to do, that is, besides stare at the traffic and chat about the day's events with a friendly reporter from CNN.

> *Make the traffic patterns work for you.*

This is an example of a strategy that successful people have always adopted: *Live off peak*. In other words, step back and make the most intelligent choices you can when it comes to investments of time, effort, and energy — regardless of what the rest of the world is doing. Living off peak often means being willing to do work during times of the day when everyone else has gone home. But if it means you can (for instance) get far deeper background information on a hot story than your competition does, then the effort is worth it.

Living off peak means taking a different approach than the crowd takes. In essence, it means making a habit of scheduling your day to make the traffic patterns of others work for you. For instance, I spend well over half my working time on the road. My time is valuable, so I've come to the conclusion that it doesn't make a lot of sense for me to stand in a long checkout line waiting for an up-to-date receipt to give to my accounting people when I make it back to the New York office. So instead of checking out at 12 noon, when everyone else is lined up, I make a call down to the front desk and request a late checkout. That gives me an hour or two more to work in my room — and I spend zero time fighting traffic in the lobby. Let me tell you, that hour or two adds up over 150 hotel trips a year!

Here's another example of how living and working off peak can pay off. A couple of years ago, I got a call from my publisher informing me that a major consumer products company had purchased 400 copies of my book on cold calling for distribution to its sales force. Clearly, this company was a good candidate for an in-person sales training program! I reached the person who had placed the order, and learned that the book was indeed "required reading" throughout the company. In order to get a decision about a training program, though, I'd have to talk to the vice president of sales and marketing — and at the time I called, that person was out of the office. So I'd have to call back the next day.

Well, I called back the next day, as instructed. I gave my initial contact's name and asked to speak with the vice president of sales and marketing. Unfortunately, I ran into one of those gatekeepers whose mantra was "She's not interested." I could have been mailing out $100 bills, and this person would have informed me that his boss was "not interested" in speaking to me about how many bills she wanted me to send her. I simply could not get through to this person in the conventional way.

What would you have done in that situation? Here's what I did. I called back at 7:30 the following morning and reached the VP before the gatekeeper made it in to work. I got through to my contact and set the appointment. That's working off peak, and it's a great way to make things happen.

Another great way to work off peak is to take full advantage of voice mail. When I train salespeople, I tell them *always* to leave messages on automated message systems. You can do so at your own convenience, and you'll be taking advantage of a great way to connect with people. My favorite voice mail message for new contacts sounds like this: "Hi, Mr. Jones. This is Stephan Schiffman from D.E.I. Management Group. I'm calling regarding XYZ Company. Please call me at 212 555-5555." XYZ Company is a firm familiar to Mr. Jones — typically a company in his industry or a related industry — with which my company has done business in the past. The reason for my call is to tell the contact about the program we put together for XYZ. This message — which I can leave at 2:00 a.m. or 9:00 p.m. — yields a 75 percent return call rate! That's an off-peak strategy you should definitely incorporate into your daily routine.

Most people never take the time to figure out how to live and work off peak, and that's a shame. How many people do you know who spend so much time "following the rules" that they hardly get anything accomplished? Recently we did a training program for a bank; my contact there told me that he had the ultimate story of someone who *refused* to live and work off peak. I told him I'd heard just about every story about inefficiency, but he insisted he had a new wrinkle. He was right. That month, a woman had waited in line at his bank for half an hour — to complain about how slow the lines were.

Don't follow her example. Find ways to live off peak.

MAKE IT HAPPEN PRINCIPLE 30

Your time is too valuable to waste waiting in line.

RULE 31 Solidify Your In-Person Opening

Paul Simon, the singer, takes an interesting approach to setting his concert playlist. He always starts out with a number that's so familiar to him he can almost perform it on "automatic pilot." That allows him to get his bearings, establish rapport with the audience, and make any adjustments he needs in his style or delivery. In other words, he picks a song that's incredibly familiar to him, so he doesn't have to think about the song itself while he connects with his audience.

133

Exactly the same principle applies to the very opening of your meeting with a new contact. When I meet with a contact for the first time, I rely on a "song" that's so familiar to me that I can execute it almost without thinking. At the same time, I'm evaluating everything around me — the contact, the company, the surroundings, the level of activity of employees — and thinking about what I need to do next to move forward with this person in the buy-in process.

Earlier, we talked about the importance of identifying the first question you plan to ask the contact. That's essential, and that question may change from person to person. Here, I'm going to walk you through the "opening number" I use to *get* to that question, and the questions that follow it. In essence, this is the portion of the relationship where I move from the opening to the information phase of the buy-in process.

> *Selling an idea is simply a matter of listening to what the other person reveals.*

I'm going to assume now that you're on a first meeting, and that you have the objective of setting a second appointment at the conclusion of that meeting. If your contact agrees to a second meeting, you know that person's probably serious about playing ball with you. In my experience, if you use the strategies outlined for you in Rules 26, 27, and 28, it's relatively easy to schedule a first appointment; the real test of whether you've connected with someone who's playing ball with you is winning a commitment for a scheduled *second* meeting.

At the *very* beginning of any meeting, what is the first thing that happens between the people involved? Small talk!

Banter or small talk is an integral part of any relationship, particularly any *new* relationship. The early portion of the meeting allows you to learn more about your prospect as an individual and establish commonality with that person. You may find out that you attended the same college, or like the same sports teams, or dislike coffee. The small-talk period also gives you the opportunity to make some important observations. Does this person appear anxious, have a sense of humor, speak quickly, or seem well informed?

A good all-purpose opening question during the small-talk phase is, "I'm just curious. How long have you been with XYZ Company?" Or "What were you doing prior to becoming the VP of marketing?" Of course, you can also talk about sports, the weather, or interesting objects in the room.

The actual small talk comes pretty easily to most people. The challenge is the transition. After a few moments of small talk, there's a really big pause.

Then, after that pause, it's very easy to do something silly — namely, say something the other person has heard a thousand times already, like:

"Okay, let's get down to business."

"Thanks so much for seeing me; here's how I thought we might begin. I'd like to discuss A, then B, and so on."

"Well, shall we get started?"

Automatically, the meeting is off to a bad start. The caller hasn't differentiated her company, and has placed all the focus on herself, which is a big mistake. (See Rule 32.) Here's what I do instead. I use a transitional phrase that eliminates that awkward pause, puts the other person at ease, and lays the groundwork for what's going to follow. This is the link from talking about the person's early career, or admiring the pictures on the wall, to talking business. Once you decide that it's time to move on, you're going to ask your prospect:

"Before we get started, would it help if I told you a little bit about what we do?"

The other person will most likely *not* be familiar with your company, and will respond positively to hearing about it. By the way, if the contact says that it would be better to talk about a specific challenge he or she is facing, let the person do so — and take notes! But in most cases, you'll find that the person will say, "Sure, go ahead." You've removed the pressure from the transition.

Then you're going to give a brief "commercial" for you and your organization — one that describes what you do in general terms and does *not* offer recommendations for the other person's situation. Remember, you have not yet gathered any information! Your aim here is to move seamlessly into the second phase of the buy-in process, that of gathering information. And you're going to use a mini-commercial, perhaps one adapted from the material you developed under Rule 11, to do that. Your commercial is going to close with a brief question that silently initiates the information-gathering process.

This transition is extremely important. If you handle it correctly, it will not only begin the information-gathering phase for you, but will also help you establish strong nonverbal rapport with the other person. You're taking the pressure off *and* assuming a certain measure of responsibility for the meeting. More to the point, since you know your opening cold, you're watching the other person for signs of interest, and "pitching" your message carefully so as not to deliver your commercial too quickly, too slowly, too loudly, or too softly. Establishing good non-verbal rapport is one of the most vital jobs you have at the outset of a meeting with a new contact. (It's estimated that nonverbal communication accounts for 65 percent of the perceived content of a conversation, while verbal communication accounts for 35 percent of the content.)

Here's what the sequence might sound like after the small-talk portion concludes. Look at it carefully.

"Mr. Jones, would it help if I told you a little bit about myself and Trans-Line Information Services?"

"Yeah, that's a good idea. Why don't you do that?"

"Okay. We're the fifth-largest data carrier in the industry; we have $3 billion in annual revenue. We operate a nationwide switch-based network, and we develop customized programs for more than 4000 companies. Our client list includes companies like Acme, Beltway, Criteria, and Domino. I've worked for Trans-Line for about four years now; I started out as a senior service technician and I'm now vice president of midmarket development. You know, Mr. Jones, I was looking over my records before this meeting, and one of the things I noticed is that you're not on our customer list. I'm just curious — why not?"

Once the small-talk portion of the meeting concludes, that's what your "opening number" should look like. You should have that minicommercial down cold! Notice once again that the commercial concludes with the first question of the interview phase of the buy-in process.

Please take a few moments now to write down your own commercial and a sample concluding question on a separate sheet of paper. Do this before continuing with the book.

MAKE IT HAPPEN PRINCIPLE 31

Get your opening meeting sequence — a minicommercial and a concluding question — down cold.

RULE 32 — Know Where You Add Value

A few years ago, I was scheduled to give a presentation to a gigantic prospective customer. I was up against three huge competitors. All four companies were scheduled to make their "pitch" on the same day.

My three competitors used PowerPoint graphics and sound effects and huge screens and various other technical marvels to highlight what they thought they could do for the prospective customer. They took no notes. Apparently, they came to talk.

When my turn came, I pulled out a yellow legal pad and a pen and asked, "What are you trying to do with this program?" There was a pause. The senior member of the group said, "Steve, do you realize you're the only person to ask us that today?"

I got half an hour's worth of notes about what that company was trying to accomplish. I also got that sale. Even though my meeting was not as flashy as my competitors', I was focused on the *do* — and they weren't.

> *You're not selling your idea to "a company." You're selling it to individual people by asking them exactly what they're trying to accomplish.*

Think for a moment about what happened during that meeting. How could a yellow legal pad beat not one, not two, but three full-blown multimedia presentations that included all the bells, whistles, and animated displays you can imagine?

The answer is simple. Taking notes on an old-fashioned yellow legal pad sends a much different message than bombarding people with PowerPoint demonstrations, e-mail attachments, and brochures.

Of the following possible questioning objectives, which would you say is the most important?

1. Determining how many PowerPoint slides you can fit into a one-hour meeting.

2. Determining whether the other person has read your previous written correspondence or e-mail in detail.

3. Determining whether the other person uses the same spreadsheet that you do.

4. Determining the names of the other person's children for entry into your smart phone.

5. Determining what the other person is trying to accomplish.

The correct answer, of course, is objective 5. But so many businesspeople focus on issues related to objectives 1 through 4 that you have to wonder whether technology has really moved us forward all that much.

Identifying what the other person is trying to accomplish is vitally important — far more important than the graphics in your e-mail attachment, the size of your computer, or the display options on your software. As for asking questions about the prospect's family, that may be one effective form of small talk, but it certainly should not be the driving force at your business meetings.

So what did I know before I walked in the door?

Remember, I asked a very simple question: *What are you trying to do with this program?*

I knew that *asking* what the company does was smarter than *assuming* what it "needed"! Once you're ready to ask what the prospect does, a low-tech approach is actually better — or, at the very least, far more flexible — than a high-tech sell.

Why? Because writing things down is a great way to fight your temptation to recite everything you believe you can offer the prospect. Taking notes not only gives you great information, it also encourages your prospect to open up to you. Your aim is to send a nonverbal signal that you are ready to pay attention and ready to do business. By taking out your notepad and pen at the beginning of the meeting, you send a silent signal: "What you are telling me is worth writing down." That puts the other person in a position of high status. Paradoxically enough, it also puts you in ultimate control of the meeting. You're the master of ceremonies! When you're given important information, you can lean in closely and write more quickly on your pad. When you're given obviously confidential data, you can demonstrate your discretion by not writing for a few moments. When you're asked about one of your company's products or services, you can support your answer with impromptu diagrams. (These can be very effective!)

When you take notes, you are in a position of authority; at the same time, you are putting the other person in a position of high status. To maintain that position of authority, do not ask for permission to take notes during your meeting with the prospect. Simply take the initiative, pull out the pad, and start writing.

MAKE IT HAPPEN PRINCIPLE 32

Low-tech selling means asking what the company does, determining what it's trying to accomplish, and writing everything down.

33 Ask About the Past, the Present, and the Future

A while back, my mother went to an electronics store. She stepped up to the counter, caught the eye of a counter attendant, and said, "I want to buy a CD player."

The person at the counter said, "You've come to the right place. Let me show you what we have." And with that, the clerk did what just about everyone at these kinds of stores does: He demonstrated a couple of different models at a couple of different price ranges. He recited a memorized list of features so rapidly that the average consumer could not possibly keep up. My mother selected one of the models, paid for it, and went home.

Later that week, I asked her how she was enjoying her purchase. She told me that she wasn't all that happy with it. When I asked her why, she said, "It doesn't do what I want it to do."

I asked her to explain exactly what she meant. My mother reminded me that she had been hoping to find a CD player that could play for three or four hours continuously. She entertains quite a bit, and she found the constant interruptions in her conversations to change the CD player to be annoying.

My point is that the salesperson she talked to should have done something other than simply show her his top three models of the day. He should have stepped back and asked her some questions. For instance:

- What made you decide to visit our store today?

141

- What kind of music system do you currently own?
- How do you plan to use the system you want to buy?

That first question — "What made you decide to visit us?" — focuses on the past. It would have given the salesperson a look at the recent (or distant!) history that affected my mother's decision to walk into the store in the first place.

The second question — "What are you using now? — would have given the salesperson a look at what my mother was doing presently.

The third question — "What are your plans for the future?" — would have shown the salesperson how my mother was hoping to use the system she planned to buy. This question of *using* is particularly critical. Too many people (like this salesperson) focus on the quick kill, the immediate match. The development of good long-term relationships depends on understanding how the other person can actually benefit from *using* what you have to offer.

Three simple questions. That's just the beginning of the line of inquiry the salesperson should have initiated with my mother. Those three will do for a start. In order to gather enough information to build a plan that really makes sense for a customer, you must ask about the *past*, the *present*, and the *future*. That's one of the prerequisites of successful completion of the second phase of the buy-in process, the information-gathering phase.

Instead of taking the time to discover what my mother had done in the past, was doing now, and planned to do in the future, the salesperson took the so-called easy way out of the conversation. He made a recommendation based on no information whatsoever.

> *When someone discusses his or her goals with you, you have an opportunity to build a relationship. Don't waste that opportunity by making a premature recommendation.*

Any time you speak to a potential business ally — a prospective employer, a potential customer, a likely distributor of your products, someone who can help your services reach a new market — ask about the past, the present, and the future. Any idea you build a plan around must take into account the answers you receive. Remember: In order to move forward to the third phase of the buy-in process, you must present what makes sense to the other person — that is, something that will help the person accomplish what he or she is looking to do. What you are hoping to accomplish is immaterial to the other person. Only by exploring the past, the present, and the future can you hope to gather the information you need to move forward to the next phase of the relationship.

MAKE IT HAPPEN PRINCIPLE 33

The best way to build a relationship is to explore what people have done in the past, what they are currently doing, and what they plan to do in the future.

RULE 34

34 Ask "How" and "Why" Questions

Eileen, a recently hired personnel director, was frustrated. "These job applicants are all lying to me!"

I asked her what she meant. It turned out that, during her discussions with applicants, she would ask questions like "Have you got experience in evaluating vendors?" The candidate would offer an answer in the affirmative, and Eileen would ask a follow-up question that the person seemed to handle well. Eileen would then duly schedule the person for a second interview with a manager at the firm. Only then would it become clear that the applicant was taking a half-ounce worth of experience and passing it off as a 10-pound qualification. Now Eileen wanted to know what she could do to match people with opportunities more effectively, and she sought my advice.

Here's what I told her:

- Any new contact has, by definition, no relationship with you.
- The quality of the information you receive tends to improve as the relationship grows and matures. That means the information you get in the very early stages of any new relationship may not be completely accurate. (Salespeople encounter this problem all the time.)
- By focusing questions on how and why (rather than whether), you can instantly determine a new contact's level of knowledge and experience. If this person isn't "who" you're looking for, you'll find out immediately!

Eileen began interviewing much more effectively. She started asking questions like "How did you select vendors in your previous job?" and "Why did you take that approach?" When she saw applicants begin to stammer and stutter in response, she knew that, no matter what the person *claimed* to be responsible for, his or her actual knowledge base did not reflect the depth of experience that Eileen was looking for.

The same principle can be applied to many other business situations involving new contacts. For instance, before we walk in the door for a meeting with a contact, we often have to be able to identify whether this person actually has decision making authority in a given area. Most people in this situation attack the problem by simply asking, at some point, "Do you make decisions in this area?" The direct approach is usually a mistake.

As Eileen's story suggests, asking "Are you in charge of these kinds of decisions?" is unlikely to get you the information you want, especially when you ask it early in the relationship. In fact, you'll quite often get a totally inaccurate response. Why? Because the other person has not built up any trust with you yet. In fact, it's quite common for people to reply, "Oh, yes, I make the decisions in that area," even when they don't. Perhaps they're covering for a busy boss. Perhaps they want to appear more important than they actually are. Whatever the reason, asking, "Are you in charge of decisions in Such and Such an area?" usually doesn't work.

Instead, prepare yourself, before the meeting begins, to ask an even better question. At some point during the meeting, you're going to say something like this:

"How did you end up working with XYZ Company?"

"Why did you choose to set up your marketing program that way?"

145

"How did you determine whether that initiative was successful?"

If the person you're talking to has no idea how to answer your questions, guess what? You're not dealing with the person you should be dealing with! And the beauty of this approach is that, having posed the question, you now have a great reason to work with your contact so as to include the actual decision maker — the "who" you're looking for — in your discussions. You have to track down the how and the why to put together your plan!

> *Ask the how and the why — and the who will emerge.*

The point in the discussion where you feel comfortable asking these kinds of questions will vary from contact to contact. You should be prepared to ask them, however.

By the way, "how" and "why" variations on questions are highly effective throughout the second phase of the buy-in process — not just when you're trying to identify a specific decision maker within a target organization. Be ready to ask questions like "Why do you do it like that?" and "How did you decide that was important?" even *after* you've identified the right "who."

MAKE IT HAPPEN PRINCIPLE 34

Asking "how" and "why" questions is the best way to find out who handles decisions in a given area.

146

RULE 35 Spend at Least 75 Percent of Your Time Gathering Information

Here's a transcript of a radio exchange that took place off the coast of Newfoundland some years ago between the captain of an American naval ship and a Canadian naval officer.

American captain: Recommend you alter your course 20° to the north in order to avoid collision.

Canadian officer: No. Recommend you alter *your* course 20° to the south in order to avoid collision.

American captain: Perhaps I haven't made myself clear. This is the captain of a U.S. Navy ship. I repeat: Recommend you alter *your* course.

Canadian officer: Impossible. You must alter *your* course.

American captain: You are speaking to the captain of the *U.S.S. Missouri.* We are a large warship of the United States Navy. Strongly recommend that you alter your course *immediately.*

Canadian officer: Captain, this is a lighthouse. Do as you see fit.

> *You cannot sell an idea through intimidation, manipulation, or coercion. A plan that doesn't make sense is a plan that doesn't make sense, even if you outline it in a more intense tone of voice.*

Sometimes, when we haven't taken the time to gather the right information, the recommendations we make are downright ludicrous. Let me illustrate that principle as it applies in business settings — by telling you about three people who came into my office recently.

The first meeting was with a bright-eyed man in his early twenties who was selling advertising for local businesses. I noticed him waiting in the reception area and remembered that he had scheduled an appointment with me for that day. Time allowing, I will meet with just about anyone — once.

I stopped, introduced myself, and said, "We'll be meeting in a couple of minutes." He said, "Yes, I know, I'm looking forward to it." (Actually, we were meeting at that very moment, but there he was, nodding his head vigorously in agreement. I guess this exchange tells you something about what you can do when you take the role of authority figure in a business setting.)

"Before we actually meet," I continued, "let me ask you something. What's the single most important question you plan on asking me today? What's the first thing you're going to ask me?"

He sat there in silence for a moment. Then he said solemnly, "Well, Mr. Schiffman, the most important thing for me to find out today is whether your current advertising is working for you. What do you like about it — and what would you change about it if you could?"

Our "actual" meeting lasted about five minutes. He led with that question. I told him I wasn't doing any advertising at all, and thus could not go into much detail about whether it was working for me. He didn't get the sale.

The second meeting was with a telecommunications consultant who came in to see me regarding the phone system in our office. Here's what he asked to start out

148

our conversation: "Are you happy with your telephone system?"

Interestingly, that meeting also lasted about five minutes. There really wasn't much to say! After all, I was "happy" with my current phone system. When I picked up the phone, I heard a dial tone. When someone had to get in touch with me, the phone rang. Certainly I wasn't *unhappy* enough to take the initiative myself to make any change. I did not end up doing business with that telecommunications consultant.

The third meeting was with a job applicant, someone who wanted to work for me as a salesperson. When this young woman sat down for her interview, I began, "Tell me — what's the single most important question you're going to be asking me today?" Can you guess what she said? She wanted to know how much money I planned to pay her.

She didn't get the job offer.

Although it may seem as though these three people were asking me questions, I'm not so sure that's what they were actually doing. However you describe what they were doing, all three of them failed to make something happen — because all three fell prey to a basic fault in relationship-building strategy. They failed to ask a simple "do-based" question, the kind that would instantly let them know exactly where they stood with me — and what they should ask me about next.

The kind of question I'm talking about would have encouraged me to open up about my company. It would have allowed each of these people to spend most of the conversation *gathering information meaningful to the person on the other side of the table.*

When I'm developing a new relationship, or exploring an opportunity within an old one, my goal is to spend 75 percent of the buy-in process in the information-gathering stage. I set that standard for myself — and train it into everyone who attends our programs — because it is *extremely easy* to ask questions that close off the exchange. We're always tempted to "ask questions" that simply reflect our own assumptions about the situation. But if you make a conscious effort to spend three-quarters of your time in the second phase of the process, you're less likely to let these kinds of short-sighted questions determine the plan you eventually put together for the other person.

In fact, if you translate them properly, these impulsive queries are not questions at all. Take another look at the three "questions" each of my conversational partners posed. What were they really saying? "You should make the Yellow Pages part of your current advertising program." (What if I don't have an advertising program?) "I suspect you're unhappy with your current telephone system." (What if I thought I was happy with what I bought last year?) "I'm interested in earning a good salary with your firm." (What if I'm more interested in the value you can add to my company?)

Do-based questions are much better at helping you expand your information-gathering phase. They're a superior platform from which to build the relationship. Consider how differently all three of those conversations would have gone if each of the people involved had focused on what my company was actually *doing*.

The Yellow Pages representative could have said, "Mr. Schiffman, I checked my list this morning, and I noticed that you're not advertising in the Yellow Pages. So I'm just wondering, why not?" (See Rule 29.) He'd have learned exactly what, if anything, had kept me from advertising in the past, and he'd be in an excellent position to learn what kind of program I might be open to discussing. He'd find out my thinking — my story. Presumably, that's what he wants to build his plan around. So it's worth knowing!

The phone consultant could have said, "Mr. Schiffman,

I see by the phone here on your desk that you're using the Acme brand phone system in your office now. I'm just curious. How did you pick that system?" He'd have taken advantage of an obvious cue — the phone on my desk — and learned what went into my company's decision to purchase Acme. Again: worth knowing!

How about the job applicant? Perhaps you're thinking that she had no such information to build a question around. Quite the contrary! She knew that I was interviewing job applicants. Accordingly, she could have built a do-based question around that fact. "Mr. Schiffman, I'm just wondering: What's behind your decision to interview people for this position? What's happened recently to make you look for someone — and what are you trying to get accomplished with this hire?"

You've just seen three examples of do-based questions that support the emerging relationship. If you learn to master the impulse to "sell, sell, sell," you can begin your discussions by asking fundamental questions like these and following up. You'll find that people will open up to you and give you all the information you need. Make it your goal to spend 75 percent of each buy-in process working in the information-gathering phase. Once you've found an appropriate do-based opening, continue to explore what the person on the other side of the desk does. Take plenty of notes. Ask about the past, the present, and the future. Ask about how and why. And always remember the captain who faced down that lighthouse in Newfoundland. Put in the time. Do your level best to avoid making recommendations that have nothing whatsoever to do with reality.

MAKE IT HAPPEN PRINCIPLE 35

You should spend at least 75 percent of the buy-in process in the second stage — the information-gathering step.

RULE 36

Verify Before Recommending Anything

Back in the early 1900s, an escape artist was performing one of his seemingly death-defying stunts in an English vaudeville theater. The trick involved undoing a pair of handcuffs, wriggling free from a series of ropes, exiting from a canvas bag, and sneaking out from a hidden panel set into a large shuttered box. The escape expert completed all his maneuvers in record time — snuck through the secret compartment through a special passageway that led beneath the stage — and prepared to make his way around to the back of the house for his triumphant surprise entrance.

Unfortunately, he forgot for a moment that he was working that evening in a building that housed not one but *two* active theaters, each featuring a different show. When he burst through the doors and ran down the aisle shouting, "Here I am!", the audience stared at him in apparent shock. Disoriented, he checked the stage and realized that he had blundered into the wrong theater — and interrupted a tense murder mystery at the very instant that the identity of the killer was about to be revealed.

Suppose the escape artist had taken a moment to double-check his situation before hurtling through those doors in triumph? If he'd taken just a little time to verify his assumptions before committing himself, he would have saved himself a lot of embarrassment — and spared that audience one of the strangest entrances in theatrical history.

The escape artist had done everything right, everything he should have done, right up to the point where he started toward "his" audience. At that point, he was directionally challenged — but he didn't know it. Moving from the second phase of the buy-in process to the third phase can be similarly tricky. Before we make any recommendation, before we present the plan we think will make sense to the other person, we have to build in some kind of verification process. That gives us the chance to incorporate previously ignored facts, revise any inaccuracies, and make a last-minute course correction if we need to. As the story of the escape artist illustrates, last-minute course corrections can be essential!

As the diagram shows, verification constitutes a substep between the second and third phases of the buy-in process. It allows us to take the information we've got, confirm it, and make sure we're pointed in the right direction.

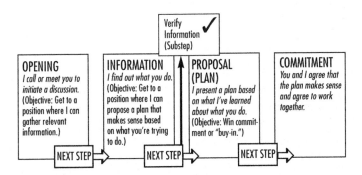

One way to verify your information is simply to review, verbally, all the key assumptions you anticipate building your plan around. You might say, "Ms. Chen, based on what you've told me so far, this is what I'm hearing."

That's the beginning of verbal verification. There's another way to approach the verification substep, though, and I think it's much more effective. Before I make any formal recommendation, I verify all my information by using a preliminary presentation. This is a brief outline that the prospect gets to scribble all over. I want that to happen! The prospect's notes serve as the basis of my formal written presentation. It's a very powerful tool.

Basically, an outline is a document that says, "I am not a proposal." This is my opportunity to come back with ideas about pricing, timing, and specific products and services that could help the prospect attain the goals we discussed together in the first meeting. The outline is a document that makes it much easier for me to course-correct *before* I make a formal recommendation. It lets me gain clarification on the information I've gathered thus far.

My experience is that the outline provides you better information than any kind of verbal verification, because people are generally more comfortable offering "constructive criticism" while reviewing a written document than they are contradicting something you've just said. And the aim here is to be corrected, be righted, by the other person, so that you can move into the third step of the buy-in process. (For more information on the vital importance of "being righted" by the other person, see Rule 40.)

Whether your verification process takes place through a written document or a conversation, it should confirm all the important assumptions about the emerging relationship. Be sure to verify:

- The fact that your contact is in a position to make the decision for you *or* help get the decision made for you.
- The fact that the main points of the plan you're about to develop "make sense" — that is, match up with what the other person is trying to accomplish.
- The dollar amount under discussion.
- The timetable for implementation.

All these issues must be addressed directly *before* you make any formal recommendation. If there's a problem in any of these areas, you will want to know about that problem sooner rather than later. The outline is a great way to get that information out on the table.

Here's an example of what an outline, or preliminary proposal, looks like. Note that it is extremely brief.

COMMUNICORP SERVICES OUTLINE: PRELIMINARY PROPOSAL
Prepared Exclusively for Mike Deacon, XYZ Company

Overview: XYZ Company is a dynamic, fast-growing firm dedicated to delivering superior widget repair services to small businesses. The company also secures referrals for later upgrades to on-site widget management equipment, which it sells. Communicorp is one of the fastest growing communications companies in America. As a direct result of working with Communicorp, clients such as Acme Products, Cogsworth Financial, and Basso Inc. have simplified their billing, secured highly competitive rates, and increased internal efficiency through speedy, easy access to the Internet.

KEY OBJECTIVES FOR XYZ
- Simplify billing; free up time so less hours spent analyzing long distance expenses
- Provide accessible summaries of departmental calling patterns via hard and soft copy for circulation to XYZ senior management.
- Provide seamless, easily accessible Internet gateway to team members via dial-up.

PRELIMINARY RECOMMENDATIONS
Standardized Billing. Communicorp has the unique ability to place all services on one simple invoice detailing long distance, wireless, and Internet charges. We pride ourselves on generating invoices and call records for over 2.5 million customers every month with virtually 100% accuracy. (Communicorp has been rated in independent studies by the California PUC to have accurate and correct billing.)

Call Tracking Program. We provide invoice and Call Detail Record information via paper and disk (ASCII or print image). This makes it easy to circulate detailed tracking reports for XYZ.

OTHER ISSUES WE DISCUSSED

Directory Assistance. Communicorp provides Directory Assistance via Area Code + 555-1212.

Network Security. Communicorp utilizes 100% fiber optic transmission which has been approved for on-encryption required transmission under U.S. federal security standards. Communicorp will support customer encrypted transmissions where signals do not jeopardize network integrity.

Customer Care. Our Customer Care Center operates 24 hours a day to meet the needs of a fast-paced business environment. Our 1-888-WE-CARE number is specifically designed to provide immediate access for our dedicated customers to a specialized customer care group.

PRICING

The following is an example of some simple pricing that is currently offered to a customer with monthly long-distance usage that parallels XYZ's . The rates below assume a start date of July 31, 2000.

Dedicated T-one interstate Florida	.0XX/minute
Dedicated T-one intrastate California	.0XX/minute
Dedicated T-one intrastate Arizona	.0XX/minute
Dedicated T-one Interstate Inbound outbound	.0XX/minute
Switched Interstate Inbound Outbound	.0XX/minute
Monthly service fee for entire package	$XXXX

Some people shy away from this verifying step because they're afraid of making a mistake in front of the other person. Well, if you're *never* corrected by someone you're talking to, guess what? You're not asking the right questions — and you're almost certainly going to spend more time and energy than you should on relationships that don't go anywhere! Find out about the mismatches *before* you put together a formal recommendation. You'll save yourself time, energy, and aggravation.

Just as a lawyer never asks witnesses a question without already knowing the answer, you should *never make a formal recommendation without obtaining the contact's buy-in at the conclusion of the second phase of the buy-in process.* The other person has to get some clear signal that you intend to ask for a commitment to work together once you *do* make a formal recommendation!

> *Use the outline to let your contact know that you intend to ask for a commitment to move forward with your plan.*

If you never get any clarifying or corrective feedback from your prospects, you may be intimidating people or trying to move forward in the buy-in process too quickly. Do the responses you get become shorter and shorter, and contain less meaningful information as the relationship progresses? If so, you need to work on your willingness to be corrected!

Once you learn to verify information properly, you will find that your formal recommendation (the plan or proposal) virtually writes itself. When your outline "makes sense" to the other person, you will be ready to move into the third phase of the buy-in process. This is where you outline exactly how you propose to work together.

From there, moving to the fourth phase can (and should) be as simple as saying, "It makes sense to me. What do you think?" (See Rule 41.) If there are entirely new issues, sudden reversals, or mysterious attempts to slow down or sidestep this final phase, then you can rest assured that you have not gathered and verified all the relevant information.

MAKE IT HAPPEN PRINCIPLE 36

It's a mistake to rush into the third phase of the buy-in process before verifying your information.

RULE 37 Manage Your Opportunities Effectively

(Note: Rule 37 covers a great deal of critical information. The discussion is somewhat longer than that for other rules in the book, but the system outlined here will help you take control of your business relationships. Please read it from beginning to end before proceeding to Rule 38.)

Many years ago, one of our salespeople came in to my office on a Saturday morning to discuss what his sales picture looked like over the next month or two. He wanted my feedback on which leads were "live" and which weren't. I sat down and evaluated all his prospects, separating the active relationships from the inactive ones, and identifying subcategories within each of those two groups that clarified exactly what was on the horizon.

To get a better visual sense of what was happening — and likely to happen — in his accounts, I wrote the name of each of his contacts on a card and pinned all the cards in their various subcategories onto a bulletin board across from my desk.

An hour into the process, the sales rep had a definite picture of what the next two months looked like. As the meeting concluded, he said, "Thanks for all your help, Steve." With that, he started to take down the cards from the bulletin board.

"Wait a minute," I said. "Let's leave them up there. Let's update the cards every day, so we know exactly what's going on with all the people you're talking to."

That day marked the birth of our Prospect Management System, which is now the core tool in one of our signature programs — and the primary tool I use to manage my business. (Our Prospect Management Board occupies almost an entire wall in my office.) More than 100,000 people have been trained to use the system I set up that day. Salespeople around the world use the system to track prospects; managers and executives use it to keep track of new business alliances. *Anyone who must win commitments from others can use this system to track the progress of those commitments.*

The Prospect Management System breaks the buy-in process down into its constituent parts. It closely measures what's happening in your business relationships, and shows you exactly what you want to make happen *next* in those relationships. It uses different categories to give you a visual summary of all the leads you're working on. Although the system was initially designed for use by salespeople, it has been adapted to many other business settings with great success. (In the following discussion, for simplicity's sake, I'm going to refer to people who are "playing ball" with you — that is, actively discussing the possibility of working with you — as "prospects," whether or not you sell for a living.)

Let's look at the Prospect Management Board now.

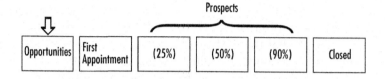

Reading from left to right we have Opportunities, First Appointments, three Prospects categories (25, 50, and 90 percent) and Closed.

On one end of the board is the Opportunities column. Opportunities aren't prospects yet; they're the people or companies we *want* to do business with. They could be people we still haven't called. They could also be people we've talked to in the past but currently have no active discussions with about potential commitments.

Not everyone we speak to is an active prospect!

Prospects are people who have agreed to work through a series of Next Steps with us. If a contact hasn't made any kind of commitment, then he or she is placed here, in the Opportunities column. We may also refer to these people as Candidates, Suspects (that is, people we suspect may be able to use what we have to offer), Leads, or Referrals. All these groups are a vitally important part of the system (as you'll see in Rule 46), but they're not active.

Understand, though, that the situation can change at any moment. The board is constantly updated, and the aim is always to find out *what level of commitment really is there* with any given prospect — and how that commitment reflects the likelihood of winning a commitment from the prospect.

Unfortunately, it's easy for people to fool themselves into thinking that they're talking to a prospect when they really aren't. Someone who ends a conversation by suggesting that we call again at some vague point in the future is not a prospect. Someone who told us last month that she was very interested in talking to us, but won't take our call now, is not a prospect. Someone who tells us he wants to talk to the president about working with us, but won't commit to us to schedule a follow-up call, is not a prospect.

If contacts will not "play ball," regardless of where they are in the system, they will fall back and become Opportunities. Therefore, the Opportunities column is also known as the Fallback column.

You want to develop new contacts constantly, spend as much time as you can with *active* prospects, and develop a sense of how long it takes for a formal buy-in commitment to develop from one of those prospects. *The longer a prospect spends on your board once that average time to buy-in has elapsed, the worse your chances of winning a commitment from that prospect become.*

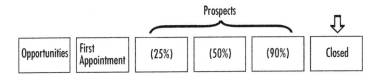

At the other end of the board is the Closed column. Well, we know what that group is. These are the companies or people who've committed to work with us. They've agreed to use what we have to offer. This is confirmed business — but of course the people in this column may also represent chances for additional commitments.

To the right of the Opportunities column is the First Appointments (FA) column. These are people with whom we've scheduled an initial appointment. We haven't yet met with them. When we make a first appointment, our opportunity moves into the FA category. Even though a first appointment is not considered an active prospect, this is still a very important column. Your job is to determine, through your ratios, how many appointments you need to bring in the commitments you require — and then maintain the FA column at that level at all times.

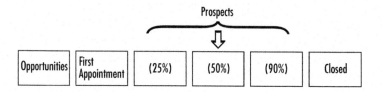

Let's look now at the key prospect columns in the middle of the board, beginning with the 50 percent category. If a prospect reaches this point, we have a 50/50 chance of closing the sale. This is the yes-or-no point where the sale could go either way.

When a prospect reaches the 50/50 category, that's not an arbitrary decision on our part. "Feelings" about the prospect don't count. There are strict criteria to have a 50 percent prospect. Before placing any prospect in the category, you must be absolutely sure that you control each of the following elements:

1. *Decision.* You're talking to the right person. In other words, you are in current discussions with the actual decision maker or someone who can get the decision made for you.

2. *Plan.* The plan "makes sense." This means whatever you are proposing fits into what the prospect is looking to do. This relates to the principle of selling an idea by finding out what the other person does.

3. *Pricing.* You know the pricing will work for both sides. Of course, the final pricing of every element of your proposal may not yet be settled. Still, it is important to discuss a basic pricing framework before placing the prospect in the 50 percent category.

4. *Timetable.* There are two critical times that both the salesperson and the prospect must understand: the decision date and the switchover date of the service. These elements are crucial, and they must be within the normal sales cycle.

5. *Next Step.* You and the prospect agree on when you will next discuss where things are going. Remember, without a scheduled Next Step, you don't have a prospect, but an opportunity.

(Do the first four elements above look familiar? They should. They're the same items your preliminary proposal or outline is meant to confirm. Prospects in the 50 percent category have passed the verification step. See Rule 36.)

When all of the above is true about a prospect, you can assume that the relationship has a 50 percent chance of resulting in a commitment. This is the make-or-break category, the one that drives the entire system. Be sure you review these five criteria closely before attempting to assign prospects to categories.

Often, we forget about average selling cycles. That means we may place prospects in the 50 percent category who don't belong there. Someone who promises to work with us six months from now, for instance, should go back into the Opportunities column, and not into 50 percent, even though that person may meet all the other criteria. Too many things can happen over the course of that six months for us to be able to count on income from this person.

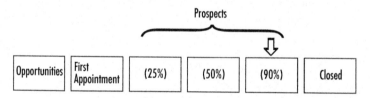

Prospects in the 90 percent category have made a verbal agreement to do business with us. The commitment is viewed as 90 percent because there is still a chance for the deal to fall through, even though the "right person" may be saying yes. Prospects in this category are also described as "contract on desk." The Next Step criterion still applies here — we have to have an established date and time to complete the formalities. After everything's signed, the prospect may be moved to the Closed column.

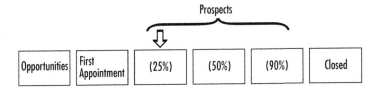

On the way to the 50 percent category is the 25 percent category — the first of the three Prospect columns, to the left of 50 percent. This column represents prospects that are currently in discussion — past the appointment stage, and in agreement with a Next Step — but that do not meet all the 50 percent criteria.

The only mandatory element of being a 25 percent prospect is having met with the salesperson and having scheduled a Next Step. Our objective for these prospects is to get them to meet all the 50 percent criteria.

The Prospect Management Board *must* be date-driven. The date of the first appointment should be noted on all cards, except opportunities. If cards are too old, they will become stale and drop off. If there are no new dates you will want to add new ones or there will be a drop in activity soon.

Here's the ideal board formation.

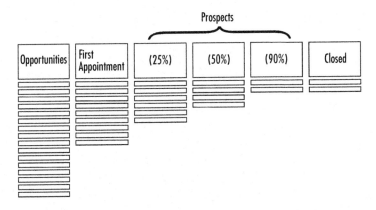

This is how you want your board to look. Many people get distracted by that Closed column, and talk themselves into thinking that the best possible formation is one in which there is lots of current business, and less to worry about in the categories to the left. Actually, that formation is a disaster waiting to happen! It means you haven't been prospecting, haven't been reaching out to people. Once your current commitments go away, you'll have nothing.

If you understand that, you can really understand the whole system. You can see that not all your prospects will make it from start to finish, and that you always want to have the FA column filled up. So the formation that is heavy in FAs, and lighter in each successive category, is an excellent formation. You're setting up appointments and prospecting proactively for new commitments. If you maintain this formation, you will have a constant stream of activity.

By familiarizing yourself with the categories and using the Prospect Management System on a daily basis, you'll gain deeper insight into your own typical buy-in process. You'll make better distinctions about the people who are (or aren't) playing ball with you. You'll instantly spot problem relationships — they'll be the ones that stay in one category for long periods of time, or don't conclude within your usual activity cycle. You'll know what's happening, with whom, at a glance. And you'll know in which relationships you have the best chance of making something happen before lunch!

You can assemble your own Prospect Management Board just as I did, with a stack of three-by-five cards and a large bulletin board divided into segments.

MAKE IT HAPPEN PRINCIPLE 37

By learning, practicing, and using the
Prospect Management System, you can manage
your opportunities effectively.

RULE 38

Build Your Schedule Around the Board

Someone once asked General George C. Marshall to identify the traits of successful people. His illuminating seven-point list is summed up below:

- Reading only summaries of reports, rather than the "long-winded" documents themselves.
- Reading quickly and committing to constant improvement of one's reading skills.
- Not spending time reviewing decisions that have already been made, but focusing instead on the best ways to implement decisions.
- Expanding one's base of knowledge relevant to current problems.
- Beginning the day early in the morning.
- Taking a nap in the middle of the day.
- Not allowing oneself to worry.

That's an excellent list! I would add only one item to the general's outline. My eighth principle for achievement relates to time management, and it reads as follows:

- Updating your Prospect Management Board regularly, and then building each week's schedule around your board.

You were introduced to the Prospect Management System as part of Rule 37. The beauty of that system is that, when updated regularly, it serves both as a visual summary of your current business relationships *and* as a superior time management tool. Your optimum weekly schedule will arise from the cards on your board.

> *Consistent stress is a signal that your time management skills need improvement. Build your daily and weekly schedules from your Prospect Management Board.*

Every Friday, take half an hour to update all the cards on your board. What has changed? What has moved forward? What has dropped off? What new strategies will you employ? Then take another half an hour to set down your schedule on the board for the coming week.

First and foremost, set aside daily time for your calls to new contacts. Then work through the following list, using the information on your board to formalize your time commitments for each category of activities.

What Are My Priorities?

- Scheduled first appointments with new contacts.
- Activities intended to move people in the 90 percent column into the Closed column.
- Activities intended to move people in the 50 percent column into the 90 percent column.
- Activities intended to move people in the 25 percent column into the 50 percent column.
- Closing and related activities. (This can be consolidation and wrap-up work related to a recently formalized commitment; it may also be work related to the actual delivery of your product or service. Be as specific as you can in your time allocations.)
- Special projects and tasks. (This category includes reports, administrative work, correspondence, task force assignments, and related activities. In essence, it's your "everything else" category.)

- Other/personal. (This category reflects days off, medical appointments, or other outside commitments that will affect your workweek.)

Make a Friday afternoon ritual out of this process. Do a full status review of all the cards on your board, then strategize *all* your activities for the coming week. Start with your prospecting calls, and then move on to face-to-face appointments, make-something-happen work with active prospects, and other items on the list above.

MAKE IT HAPPEN PRINCIPLE 38

By reviewing your Prospect Management Board every week, you can manage your time intelligently and set priorities.

RULE 39 Build Your Proposal Around Core Objectives

When Swifty Lazar negotiated the rights for Richard Nixon's memoirs, the superagent of superagents did a masterful job of unearthing critical information around which he could build a plan that "made sense."

In speaking with Frank Wells, who was then head of Warner Bros., Lazar learned that Wells had big plans for his book division. Up to that point, Warner Books had been strictly a paperback house; it had never issued a high-prestige hardcover of its own. Wells didn't flinch at Lazar's $2 million price tag (a headline-making sum in 1974); he saw a "name" book with the chance to draw massive amounts of publicity for Warner Books and establish it as a top-tier publisher.

Lazar moved on to discuss the plan with Howard Kaminsky, then heading Warner Books, and ran into some resistance. Kaminsky understood the importance of the book, but he was concerned about the size of the advance. He told Lazar he felt the asking price was high.

Secure in his knowledge of Frank Wells's priorities, Lazar decided to stand his ground and return to the core issue he had identified earlier in the information-gathering phase with Kaminsky's boss. "It's way high," Lazar agreed, "but buying the Nixon book will take you to a new level and put the house on the map." He must have known that, by underscoring this point, he was emphasizing his project's ability to deliver on a key goal that Wells had identified as a major priority for Warner Books. Lazar had built his plan around a core objective.

Lazar got the deal. I'd like to believe he sealed the commitment — that is, moved from the third to the fourth phase of the buy-in process — by saying something like "It makes sense to me; what do you think?" Whatever phrase he used, he *did* gain the commitment. The book was a major publishing event: a national best-seller, and a turning point for Warner Books. As it happened, Nixon's book did exactly what Lazar had promised it would do. It put Warner Books on the map.

> *Keep the other person's goals in mind and don't get sidelined.*

At our organization, we really don't like to use the term *objections* to describe the questions and challenges that people raise when we present plans on the basis of information we've gathered. We prefer to think of the questions as responses. When someone suggests that there's a problem, we feel reassured that the person is actually listening and thinking about what we are proposing. Responses give us the opportunity to move the relationship forward by examining and reexamining the core issues we've identified and verified. Responses also allow us to highlight resources that are applicable to the situation. Finally, responses allow us to gain insight into what the other person is thinking.

In dealing with responses during the presentation phase, I try to follow a simple three-step approach.

1. Identify the issues. (I ask myself: "Do I really understand the challenges this person typically faces, and how this particular challenge is affecting my contact right now?")

2. Validate the issues. (I try to figure out the real-world dimensions of the issue, then talk it through openly and honestly with the prospect. I don't run away from it or pretend it doesn't exist.)

3. Resolve the issues. (I appeal to the core objectives I've identified earlier in the process, and, when appropriate, I try to reinforce my organization's ability to deliver on those core objectives. If I find that we *cannot* deliver on objectives that the other person has identified as essential, I am frank about that too.)

One great way to resolve an issue that comes up during the presentation phase is to offer a story — or parable —

to illustrate the point you're making. The story should reinforce the core objective around which you've built your plan. For instance: "Jane Miller over at ABC Widgets initially told me she was concerned about our ability to deliver on time too. But you know what happened? I ended up beating her deadline by three full weeks. Right now, she's one of our best customers."

By building his plan around a core issue he'd identified with the head of Warner Bros., Swifty Lazar was able to make something very big indeed happen, despite some last-minute reluctance on the part of one of the decision makers. You can do the same.

MAKE IT HAPPEN PRINCIPLE 39

Be sure the plan you recommend reflects the core objectives you've identified and verified during the information-gathering phase.

RULE 40 Dare to Be Wrong

J ust about everyone has had the experience of trying to get the name of a contact at a certain organization — and not being able to do so. Here's my favorite story about overcoming that obstacle. One of our senior trainers has an innovative way of dealing with receptionists and gate-keepers who try to keep him from getting the names of contacts at target organizations. Whenever he is told that the target company "doesn't give out that information," our trainer simply calls back the next day and says, "Excuse me. Is Bob Foster the vice president of sales at your organization?" (Bob Foster, as you may have already guessed, is a name used specifically for this question.) Nine times out of ten, the same receptionist will happily answer back, "Bob Foster? No, no. Our vice president of sales is Melissa Grady."

Why does his question work? Because he knows the importance of daring to be wrong. There is a natural human tendency to correct other people. You can put that tendency to work for you by "throwing out" information you know to be incorrect — and waiting to see what comes back.

In order to be right, you must be willing to be *righted*. And in order to be righted, you must be willing to be wrong.

> *When your contact corrects you, you have the right information.*

This simple principle has extraordinary implications for those who must build business relationships with others. In my experience, moving forward in a relationship toward a commitment — that is, making something happen — is absolutely impossible if you don't have the right information. For a variety of reasons, it's often difficult to get people to volunteer the right information while the relationship is still young. So how do you get an accurate assessment of where you and the other person actually stand? You do what our senior trainer did. You throw out a "fact" and wait to see if you get corrected. Most of the time, you do.

How's that for a surprise? People who make things happen are willing to be wrong. They consciously throw out information that's designed to make the other person say, "No, that's not how it is." As a result, they get a clear picture of exactly where they are in any given business situation.

All too often, businesspeople are afraid of coming up wrong in front of another person. What a waste of time and energy! You only *gain* information when another person corrects you.

If there's a major account on someone's Prospect Management Board that looks like it's about to close, I make a point of calling the contact person up and saying, "Hi, John. This is Steve Schiffman from D.E.I. Management Group. Gino Sette, our salesperson, tells me that it sounds like we're going to do business together." What do you think happens when I make a call like that? There are only two options. Either the contact will say, "Yes, Gino and I had a great meeting — I think we're going to be able to put something together." Or the person will say, "Uh, gee, Steve, I'm surprised to hear that Gino felt that way about it, because we've still got some obstacles on our end. The pricing, for instance."

Here's the kicker: *We win in either situation!* If the person is in fact ready to buy from us, then my call serves to solidify the work that Gino has already done. If, on the other hand, there are still problems to be worked out, this call lets me know exactly what they are! Perhaps there are pricing issues that still need to be addressed. Perhaps the schedules don't mesh. Perhaps there really isn't a match in the first place, and the prospect has been too considerate of Gino's feelings to say so! We want that information, even if it's bad news. In fact, we are *particularly* keen to hear if there's bad news. If there's no chance whatsoever of a match between our organizations in the near term, we want to know about that right away so we can focus our efforts on talking to other prospects. The best sales representatives always understand this principle — which is why Gino, along with many others in our organization, constantly leaves voice mail messages asking me to make these calls!

But in order for this strategy to work, I have to be willing to be corrected. I can't beat around the bush. I can't mumble some vague pleasantry and hope to get good information from the discussion. I have to state what Next Step *I think is going to happen* — and gauge the reaction I get from the other side.

Once you understand that the power of information really does gravitate to the person who is willing to be corrected, you'll be able to put this principle to work for yourself and your organization in countless ways. For instance, if you're not certain what kind of budget you'll be working with to put a certain project together, throw out a number! See what happens. If you're not certain what a decision maker's priorities are for a given program, mention that other companies have come in with priorities A, B, and C. See what happens. If you can't get the receptionist to give you the name of the vice president of sales, call back a little later and try to "confirm" that it's Bob Foster!

Every once in a while, of course, you'll be right, and no correction whatsoever will be necessary. Just ask that trainer of ours. Once he asked whether Bob Foster was the VP of sales, and the receptionist said yes brightly and offered to connect him! (See also Rule 36, on the verification of information.)

MAKE IT HAPPEN PRINCIPLE 40

*In order to be righted,
you must be willing to be wrong.*

RULE 41

41

Say, "It Makes Sense to Me— What Do You Think?"

I read a book a month or so ago that made my jaw drop. Here's some of the advice it passed along on the best ways to secure commitments in business relationships:

- Dramatically write out a postdated personal check, payable to your contact, as an enticement to get the person to sign a contract with you — then try to slip the check secretly into a pile of papers so you can spirit it away while no one is looking.
- Sarcastically question the contact's ability to make independent decisions if he or she asks for time to talk to someone else in the organization.
- Attack the person's intelligence by suggesting that he or she won't be able to remember the information you've discussed next week, and must therefore make a decision on the spot about whether to work with you.

The sad fact is that there are plenty of "experts" out there who advocate manipulative, dishonest, abusive, and downright insulting "strategies" that supposedly help you win commitments from other people. Some of these books have sold in huge quantities. I don't know why.

These authors suggest that in order to get someone to say yes, you should pretend you're about to be fired, tell stupid and pointless stories to win sympathy, or question your contact's love for his or her spouse! Somehow, these

176

strategies are supposed to get your contact to say, "Gee, what a great business ally. I'm glad I had this meeting. Let's keep working with this person forever."

When it comes to formalizing a commitment with your contact, stay away from manipulative "tricks." They're morally repulsive and they don't work.

Instead, simply say, "Ms. Smith, this really makes sense to me. What do you think?" If you've done all the work in the three previous phases of the buy-in process, you'll get a commitment: "You know what, it makes sense to me too. Let's get started."

If, on the other hand, there's a problem you haven't uncovered yet, *this strategy ensures that you find out what that problem is.* "Actually, Steve, this doesn't really make sense to us, and I'll tell you why." The relationship is still alive! The person isn't reeling from some underhanded "closing trick" that has undone all the careful work you did in the first three phases of the buy-in process.

> *The best "closing trick" is not having to use a closing trick.*

Once you've made your formal recommendation, don't play games. Tell the truth. Let the other person know that what you've outlined really does make sense to you, and ask whether it makes sense to your contact. Then stop talking and see what happens.

MAKE IT HAPPEN PRINCIPLE 41

Avoid manipulative "closing tricks." Simply say, "It makes sense to me — what do you think?"

PART THREE

Make Something Happen by . . . Toughing It Out Until You Catch a Break

RULE 42 Beat "Bad Days" to the Punch

Every morning, on my way to work, I give myself an unfair advantage.

I know there are going to be stressful issues to deal with at work that day. I know there are going to be competitors trying to gain an inroad into our business. I know there are going to be problems for which I can't find instant solutions. But I start my day in such a way as to give myself a base of strength from which to face all these challenges.

I start my day by beating all my problems to the punch. I make a conscious choice to get lucky before anything in my workday has the chance to persuade me that I might actually be stuck in an unlucky day. In other words, I have a ritual that convinces me that today is in fact a great day — a lucky day — to be alive.

You should have a ritual too. Your affirmation may take the form of a prayer, a shared moment of hope and gratitude with your spouse or significant other, or a positive, optimistic phrase you find appealing. Whatever it is, I urge you to express your feelings about the great day you're about to have *out loud*. Speaking positive, affirmative words out loud has an uncanny way of instilling resilience, hope, and creativity when you need them most — and putting you in a position to draw on these resources as the day proceeds. I'm about to share *my* ritual, and of course you can certainly feel free to use it exactly as I do.

Here's how I beat "bad days" to the punch. Every morning, I step out onto the streets of New York and hail a cab. I get a very early start — typically I'm out waving down a cab around 6:30 a.m. That's pretty close to the time when the cabbies on the day shift start working. Whenever a cab pulls over and picks me up, I open up the door, climb in the back, and say, "Good morning! Am I your first customer of the day?" Nine times out of ten, the cabbie will say "Yes!" Then I say, "This is your lucky day! I'm going to have a great day today, and so are you. We both win. I'm a lucky person because I *say* I'm lucky, and here I am in your cab."

This always elicits a smile and a laugh. More important than that, however, this ritual puts *me* in the right mindset to begin my day.

> *The attitude you habitually display will determine the kinds of relationships you're able to initiate with others.*

Again, you don't have to mirror my cab ritual, but you should consider developing *some* habit for beginning your day that involves saying something optimistic right out loud. This really is a marvelous buffer against the challenges you'll face in the hours that follow. You'll be amazed how a simple routine like this can help you keep your head as the day moves forward.

If you build a morning ritual that involves someone else, you'll have the advantage of starting your day with a pleasant exchange with another person, which counts for a lot. What's more, you'll leave yourself open for some interesting experiences on subsequent mornings. Consider what happened to me.

A month or so ago, I was trying to flag down my morning taxi when suddenly a cab hurtled across three lanes of traffic to get to me. Now, that's not really unusual in New York City, so I didn't give the aggressive driving maneuver a second thought. I got a surprise, though, when I took my seat in the cab and asked, "Am I your first customer of the day?" The cabbie smiled at me in the mirror and said, "Yes, and you were my first customer of the day yesterday too . . . and I had a lucky day, just like you said! I got a $54 fare right after I dropped you off, so I'm planning to have another lucky day today!"

He held up a receipt for a $54 cab ride and grinned broadly. Now we *each* had a morning success ritual!

MAKE IT HAPPEN PRINCIPLE 42

Use spoken words to start your day with gratitude and optimism. Find a way to use the first 30 minutes of your day to build a firewall against the inevitable stresses and challenges that you will encounter.

RULE 43 Learn to Love "No"

Have you heard about the company that rewarded its people for getting turned down? It really happened. All the life insurance agents at a major insurance company were given a sheet of paper marked with a large grid. Each agent was asked to put an X in one of the boxes each and every time he or she got a "no" answer during a telephone prospecting call. Every agent who had collected 250 "no" answers on the grid received a $1000 bonus.

Perhaps you're wondering: Why in the world would a huge company pay its salespeople to collect as many "Thanks, but no thanks" responses as they could? How could the insurance company afford to pay out $4 for each and every dead-end response generated by phone? What was going on?

Well, if you stop to think about it, the bonus program really made perfect sense. The managers had simply acknowledged one of the immutable laws of making things happen in the business world. I call it the Law of No: *Every interaction worth saying yes to is preceded by a larger quantity of interactions in which one or both parties involved say no.*

That's true whether you're looking for a job, trying to identify the right company to acquire, recruiting a new chief executive for your company, searching for a noncompetitive Web site that reaches the exact same target audience yours reaches, or selling life insurance. In other words: As a rule, you don't pick up the phone and hear the other person say, "This is great! I'm so glad you called. When can we get started?" Will that kind of call happen *sometimes*? Sure. But in terms of setting up a long-term system for building business relationships, the Law of No is as reliable as reliable gets. You've got to work through a certain number of "no" interactions in order to get to the "yes" interaction. And because both kinds of answers are part of the same cycle, *each "no" interaction is worth a percentage of the value you receive from a "yes" interaction!*

> *Rejection is an inherent part of any process that consistently develops mutually beneficial relationships.*

Let me explain what I mean here, because it's an extremely important point. The managers at that insurance company weren't acting out of altruism or blind hope when they offered their agents a $1000 bonus for collecting 250 "no" answers. Their careful research had demonstrated clearly that the average agent who piled up 250 "rejections" would generate, not $1000, but *$10,000* in business!

How much is each "no" worth to you? Take the time to figure it out. Then *stop* counting the "yes" answers, and *start* counting the "no" answers.

The "no" answers and the "yes" answers really are interconnected. They are *all* part of the process of making something happen. Think back on the ideal formation of the Prospect Management Board (which we discussed under Rule 37).

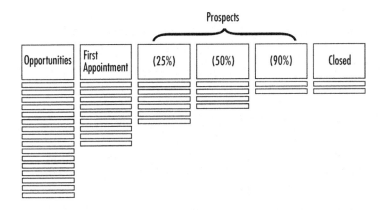

Notice once again that *people drop out of the process continuously*. No list of 100 potential customers (or companies your firm may buy, or candidates for the position of chief executive officer, or Web sites your firm could partner with) will result in 100 "yes" answers! That's the Law of No at work. In any situation where you're reaching out to new people, you've got to get a certain number of "nos" in order to get to a "yes." You have to learn to *love* "no" answers!

When we train salespeople, we tell them to look at the following ratio:

20:5:1

That translates to "20 appointments yield five prospects; five prospects yield one sale." In other words, in a typical business setting, there are 19 "no" answers for every one sale. The challenge is not to get thrown by the emotional content of those "no" answers, and to focus on the process as a whole. Once you can step back and see how everything works together, you realize that you're not all that interested in the outcome of a single call. Or a single day's calls. Or even a single week's calls. Instead, you're interested in the ongoing series of activities that *predictably* gets you past those 19 "no" answers and puts you in front of a "yes" answer, again and again and again. When you play the game long enough, you come to understand the Law of No — and you can move past the frustration connected with any individual "no" answer. Why? Because you understand that there are *always* more "no" answers in the process than "yes" answers.

Getting turned down when you ask someone to marry you, that's rejection. Getting a "no" on the telephone during your daily prospecting hour just means the system is working as it should!

MAKE IT HAPPEN PRINCIPLE 43

If you understand the Law of No, you won't get thrown by inevitable "no" answers that lead you to a "yes" answer.

44 Don't React — Respond

I believe the most important weapon in your interviewing arsenal — and your best tool for evaluating obstacles at any point in the buy-in process — is a single word.

The question to beat all questions is the simplest one of all: "Why?" A contact tells you he's considering revising his company's quarterly goals. You ask: "Why?" Another contact tells you she was never really happy with the level of attention she got from the last person she worked with. You ask: "Why not?"

Asking "Why?" is a great way to encourage another person's alert, engaged participation in a conversation. It's also one of the best ways I know to take a potentially negative exchange and transform it into a constructive dialogue that yields information you can use. When someone throws me off track — by saying something confrontational, by expressing skepticism about something we do, by making a sudden and unexpected demand — I try to use "why" questions to follow the old samurai warrior's rule: "Don't react — respond."

> *When in doubt, ask why.*

By asking why, I stand a better chance of understanding what's motivating the other person. If, on the other hand, I react heedlessly, instantly, without trying to learn anything new about the situation, I will miss out on the opportunity to learn what's really going on in the other person's head. And the less I know about what's driving the other person, the less effective I'm going to be in my task of moving the relationship forward through the buy-in process!

Unfortunately, very few people harness the power of asking why on a consistent basis. Instead, they react impulsively. For instance, during a job interview, a hiring manager comments, "I'm really not sure you're right for our company." The candidate instantly responds with "Oh, yes, I am!" and launches into a monologue about *why* he's right for the company — without having any idea what gave rise to the manager's comment in the first place. Many interviewers will make a statement like this *for the sole purpose of testing the candidate's ability to ask intelligent questions under stress.* So the "right answer" actually sounds like this: "Really? Why do you say that?"

Here's another example. Many businesspeople won't bother asking anything at all about what motivates a statement like "You know, we've usually avoided working with companies like yours." Instead of asking the obvious question — "Why is that?" — they'll just assure the contact that such a prejudice is about to change. Then they'll unfold a brochure about their company, and read that brochure word for word. What's the point of meeting with someone if all you're going to do is spout boilerplate copy instead of asking intelligent, responsive questions?

I call this kind of interaction "slapshot talk." It's not really interviewing or information gathering. It's a reaction, not an intelligent response, and it's driven by fear. When people feel challenged, they try to retain "control" of the conversation. They don't ask why. They don't try to learn anything new. They just smack whatever the person said back in the opposite direction. Picture a hockey player taking wild swings toward the net.

"We asked our current vendor to do an in-depth analysis of our senior managers' calling patterns over the past year, and we were very happy with the vendor's work."

"Oh, we could make you happier." (Slapshot!)

There's a situation practically begging for a "why" question: "Why did you want to know about your senior managers' calling patterns?"

Slapshot talk reacts; it doesn't respond. It has no use for "why" questions. It invariably offers some variation of "Hey, we've got just what you need" or "We can do that better for you" — even though "we" may know next to nothing about what the prospect actually does.

Unfortunately, the slapshot relationship model is quite common.

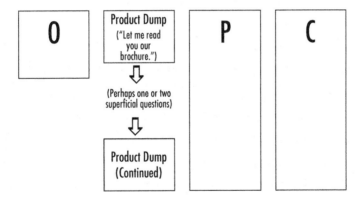

The O stands for Opening. That's followed by the "Product Dump," typically executed by reading a brochure or spec sheet verbatim to the other person. (This is also known as "throwing up" on the prospect.) The P stands for Present. and the C stands for Close. Notice how different this model is from the buy-in process; notice, too, how big that C block is. People who never ask why tend to spend a huge amount of time trying to win commitments without gathering any information. They introduce themselves, they may bat a few questions around, but they more or less instantly move in for the close. When they hit obstacles or responses they weren't expecting, they just smack the puck back toward the net — by reflex. They react. They don't respond intelligently.

In handling all the issues that the other person raises with us, we want to keep coming back to "why" questions, and explore each subject fully and completely before moving on to the next one. We don't want to sound like we are simply moving down a list of prewritten questions or memorized responses. Rather than "giving the right answer," we should seek to engage the other person in an in-depth conversation that sounds natural, flows easily, and doesn't degenerate into automated "slapshot talk."

MAKE IT HAPPEN PRINCIPLE 44

You can use "why" questions to get to the bottom of skepticism or challenge from the other person.

RULE 45 Be Willing to Walk Away

Several years ago, one of our salespeople was in a discussion with one of the world's largest consumer electronics firms. At stake was a huge series of training dates; the electronics firm was launching a brand-new

190

product and wanted help in training a newly hired group of sales reps.

As our rep worked through the buy-in process with his contact, the level of trust deepened and the quality of information improved. (That tends to happen when two people continue "playing ball" with one another for an extended period.) While he was still in the information-gathering phase — the second of the four buy-in phases — our rep asked a direct question: "Are we the only people you're talking to about this program?"

Back came the direct answer: "No, actually, you're not. We're talking to . . . " The contact then named one of our biggest competitors. The electronics firm had been speaking to this training company for quite some time. One and only one vendor would be selected to develop the new training program. And since the decision was going to be made in only a few days, our competition appeared to have the advantage. The competitor had attended more meetings, interviewed more technical people, and dealt with more top-level decision makers than we had. Apparently, we were being asked to develop a proposal so the powers that be could say that they'd looked at "multiple vendors." This is not to say that we had *no* chance of securing the deal, but the truth was that we weren't really in a position of strength.

Our sales rep said, "Oh, they won't be able to do the program for you. It's not going to work." He proceeded to outline six or seven reasons why the competitor was ill equipped to develop a training program geared to a product launch of this kind.

As valid as those reasons were, this would have been a fairly high-risk maneuver — *if* our representative had not carefully maintained his Prospect Management Board in the ideal formation. Because he did have that kind of board, he had a little more leeway when it came to contacts like this one. Do you see how he used that leeway?

Basically, by saying "It's not going to work," he was throwing the dice. He was willing to risk the possibility that this (huge) lead would drop out of his board, because he directly challenged his contact's relationship with the competition. And losing the lead was a real possibility. The contact could very well have said, "Well, *we* think it's going to work, and here's why, so why don't you just submit your proposal and we'll let you know what our decision is?" In that case, our chances for landing the deal would have dropped from slim to none.

But that was a risk our rep was willing to take, *because he had plenty of other contacts at other companies who were working through the buy-in process with him.* If this had been his only active lead, he would certainly have thought twice about challenging his contact in this way. As it stood, however, he was willing to walk away. So he threw the dice.

The dice looked pretty good when they landed. Instead of saying, "Well, *we* think it's going to work," the contact said, "Can you put all that in writing so I can show it to my boss?"

After a great deal more information gathering, and a verification step that encompassed the feedback of several people at the target company, we got the deal. We never would have, though, if our rep had been so dependent on a single lead that he'd been unable to think to himself, "I'm willing to walk away from this if I have to. Let's try something innovative here. Let's throw out the ball in a slightly different way."

> *Even if you're having a great day, a great week, or a great month, you can't afford to stop reaching out to new people. A constant stream of new business relationships gives you the freedom to say, "This isn't for me."*

There's another situation in which you have to be extremely comfortable with the idea of walking away from a contact. I'm talking about times when a contact keeps sending apparent "buy signals" but fails to move through the buy-in process within your typical time cycle. If it normally takes you three or four meetings to finalize a commitment with someone, and you're looking at a low-priority contact who is about to request her ninth meeting with you, it's time to walk away. Invest the time with a higher-priority contact who will actually move forward through the buy-in process with you.

Knowing when to walk away can be a difficult skill to master. Nonetheless, *every* highly successful person I've ever worked with has picked up the habit of disengaging from relationships that waste time, effort, and resources so as to free up time, effort, and resources for more promising relationships. Sometimes we do come across exceptional opportunities — relationships that require a little more time, a little more effort, and a little more attention. I'm not saying you should *never* invest in such relationships. All I'm saying is that you should make a *conscious choice* to do so — and be willing to cut your losses when you realize your connection with someone is not moving you toward the realization of your goals.

MAKE IT HAPPEN PRINCIPLE 45

Use your daily prospecting time to develop enough new opportunities to leave you in a position of strength. Also, if a business relationship is not moving you forward, find a way to reduce or eliminate your commitment.

46   Use Fallbacks Effectively

One of the most important challenges our training
organization faces is to convince people not to get
distracted by contacts that *sound* great, but fail to move
forward in any way. (See Rule 45.) We are constantly cajol-
ing, pleading, and, yes, begging the people we train to
focus first and foremost on the relationships that are *in
motion* — those in which the other person has demonstrated interest by "throwing the ball back" and consciously moving through the phases of the buy-in process.
In fact, my trainers and I have traded horror stories for
years about people who invested truly ludicrous amounts
of time and energy on leads that simply did not recipro-
cate any interest. Not long ago, I conducted a training program that left me in possession of the ultimate "don't let
this happen to you" story on this score. No one in our
organization has topped it, and I certainly hope no one
ever will.

During one of my training programs, I began to evaluate the Prospect Management Board of one of the participants, whose name was Ben. (Granted, *evaluate* may be
too soft a word. Others have used the word *eviscerate* to
describe this portion of our program. I admit, I can be
ruthless when it comes to getting people to be honest with
themselves about what's actually happening — or not
happening — within a relationship.)

"When did you first talk to this person?" I asked.

"Gee, I don't know — a long time ago," Ben replied.

"How long ago?"

"A while back."

194

"More than a month ago?"

"Oh, yeah, it was more than a month, definitely."

"Have you ever set a meeting with this person?"

"No, not yet — but this lead has a lot of potential, and any day now it's going to turn into a meeting."

I asked. Ben defended. I asked. He defended. On and on it went. Finally, I asked Ben to pull out his calling sheets and give me a number: the total number of times he had either talked to this contact or tried to talk to him. We took a break while he tracked this information down. Fifteen minutes later, we reconvened, and I got the total: just over *300 calls or attempted calls* to one person over a period of three months. And no appointment.

This was not exactly the most effective use of the Fallback column on Ben's Prospect Management Board! I asked, "Did it occur to you that this person may well be ducking your calls at this point?" The light of recognition crept slowly across his face, gentle as the dawn.

You'll recall that the Opportunities (Fallback) column is in the far left-hand corner of the board. It's not an active column; it's made up of the companies and people with whom we *want* to build relationships but do not yet have any kind of Next Step. Now, having a card in this column is not necessarily a negative. Fallbacks help us prioritize our time, because we can devote more energy to the prospects who *are* progressively moving through the steps. In addition, fallbacks give us the opportunity to take time and strategize with other people in our organization on the best way to get reinvolved with the person in question. Finally, moving a cherished contact from, say, a 50 percent prospect to an opportunity can serve as a much-needed wake-up call. The Fallback column alerts us to the fallen prospect's status, and it usually prompts immediate action.

That's all great. The only potential *negative* about the Fallback column is that it's so easy to become distracted by any single card we place there. Think of everything Ben could have been doing with the time he spent calling that one unproductive lead. Even if he had nothing else active on his board, he could have been calling *other* fallbacks — and setting appointments with them!

> *Repeatedly calling people who won't give you a Next Step is a sure sign of misplaced priorities.*

I hope you agree with me that Ben should certainly have reprioritized his efforts to reach that "hot lead" at some point well before the three hundredth call! Here are three simple guidelines we follow — and train others to follow — to make this kind of wheel spinning much less likely:

- Attempt to get a specific date for a follow-up call with your fallback. When the date comes around, call back and say, "Mr. Smith, this is Melanie Jones with Datapoint. When we spoke on the fourth of June about setting up a meeting, you asked me to call back today. Can we get together this coming Tuesday at three?" Throw the ball — see what happens!
- Don't phone a fallback (or any lead that is not yet a prospect) more than once a week.
- Don't phone a fallback (or any lead that is not yet a prospect) more than four times per month.

I can't tell you how many people I've met who say something like, "I'm incredibly focused on my cold calling; I make 140 calls a week," and who then turn out to be calling the same 20 leads seven times a week each!

196

Focus is great, but tunnel vision can be a dangerous thing. Tunnel vision can keep you from recognizing opportunities to make things happen in new relationships. So don't fixate on a single fallback and call it over and over again. Follow the three guidelines you've just read — and use your Fallback column effectively.

MAKE IT HAPPEN PRINCIPLE 46

Don't fixate on a single fallback.

RULE 47 Ride to the Rescue

Some years ago, I read about a major telecommunications firm that had been trying, without success, to win over a huge account. For months, the telecom firm had been dispatching salespeople, attempting to arrange meetings, and floating various creative strategies designed to win interest and attention from decision makers at the target company. So far, nothing had worked.

Then one morning there was a national news flash. One of the target company's vehicles was involved in a huge accident; there had been substantial loss of life and intense media coverage. A senior vice president at the telecommunications company knew that a time of crisis had set in. Sensing an opportunity to "do well by doing good," he arranged for a special shipment to the senior management of the company he'd been courting for so many months.

What was in the package? A hundred cellular phones — and a brief note. The note said, in essence: We understand that you need to be able to get in touch instantly with your top people now, and we hope the enclosed phones are helpful to you during this crisis.

Guess what huge company signed on as a customer the month after the accident?

One of the best ways to turn someone who says no into someone who says yes is to ride to the person's rescue when the chips are down. Is a prospective employer looking for new ideas to revive a troubled product line? Maybe a little free advice is in order. Has a potential business partner lost a key employee? Perhaps you can provide a referral. Is a businessperson you admire under attack? It's entirely possible that you may be able to pass along advice to help that person make it through the media firestorm. The point is this: If you have an opportunity to add value in an ethical and responsible way as a means of moving a stalled relationship forward, by all means take that opportunity. Use your product, your service, or your expertise in a way that delivers a benefit to and makes an impression on the contact you're trying to move through the buy-in process.

> *If you don't seize a promising opportunity to ride to the rescue of a potential ally, someone else will.*

The eighteenth-century French poet Jacques Delille once wrote: "Chance makes our parents, but choice makes our friends." He meant, I believe, that the best kind of friend — the best kind of ally — is the one you cultivate consciously. If there's a better way to do this than by coming to the aid of someone who stands to benefit from what you have to offer, I don't know what it is.

Choose many potential allies. Target them. Keep them in your Fallback or Opportunities column. When you learn that one of these potential allies has fallen on hard times or faces a challenge, be ready to saddle up and ride to the rescue.

MAKE IT HAPPEN PRINCIPLE 47

When you see an opportunity to use your product, service, or expertise in a way that can change a dormant relationship in a dramatic and constructive way, take it.

RULE 48 Break the Walls of the Aquarium

Did you know that if you place a baby shark in a glass cage that's not large enough to accommodate a full-grown shark, the shark will not grow to full size? That artificially imposed barrier will affect the shark's internal development process, and the animal will actually stop growing before it reaches the limits imposed by its surroundings.

I think all of us are in danger of surrounding ourselves with artificial barriers that can keep us from achieving at peak levels. Like the shark, we may bump up against an invisible wall or two . . . and stop growing.

There are all kinds of glass walls that keep us from attaining everything we can and should in our careers. Sometimes we erect these walls out of fear, sometimes we erect them out of boredom, and sometimes we erect them out of sheer force of habit. But we do build them, and we do pay the price when it comes to our own professional growth.

Perhaps the most dangerous invisible wall we must guard against are those we ourselves build out of complacency. When there's no crisis on the horizon, the temptation can be very strong to assume that what we're doing is more or less on target. If the president isn't mad at us, we must be doing something right! Professional growth? Higher goals? Better information? More effective techniques for reaching out to other people? Who needs them? When we bump up against these kinds of walls, we may automatically assume we've reached the limit of our capacities. Usually, we haven't.

Invisible Walls

Here are three specific examples of invisible walls I've encountered while training at some of America's top companies. Each of the three can stop a promising career in its tracks.

The "Rolodex" Wall. People who are limited by the Rolodex wall often say things like this: "I know lots of important people — so many, in fact, that all I have to do is connect with the people now in my Rolodex, and I'll never have any trouble keeping up with my competition." Here's the reality: In today's information-driven business world, our contacts change positions, careers, and industries with dizzying speed. Long-term partnerships are rare, and entire markets can change overnight. No Rolodex is ever up to date! In the twenty-first century, only those who network effectively on a regular basis will be well positioned to adapt to the constant change that is now a permanent part of daily life. *When you stop reaching out to new people, you increase your own vulnerability and the vulnerability of your organization.*

The "I Don't Have Enough Information" Wall. People limited by the information wall find themselves trapped in the comforting embrace of perpetual analysis. They try to gather 100 percent of the relevant information before attempting to initiate a new relationship or launch a new initiative. News flash: It is impossible to gather all the relevant information about any situation. Make it your aim to be right 75 percent of the time. Don't wait for all the data; take regular *action* toward your goals. Napoleon had a saying: *On s'engage et puis on voit!* ("You jump in, and then you see what to do next!") Plans are wonderful things, but they must be flexible. If the planning process inspire paralysis rather than action, it's time to change your planning habits.

> *You can never gather all the information relevant to a given situation, so don't try.*

The "Comforting Conversation" Wall. People limited by this kind of glass wall would rather talk to one pleasant, familiar contact who always says "we'll see" than talk to someone new who might say no outright to a request for a Next Step. Any "great conversation" that delivers no action, consumes your (limited) time, and keeps you from expanding your contact base is a drain on your day. Don't get hooked on these conversations. They may sound pleasant, but they actually cost you much more than you imagine.

Not long ago, a survey was conducted of what I like to call "glass-busting" salespeople — those who routinely overcome artificial, self-imposed barriers and reach high-income goals on a consistent basis: in this case, $75,000 to $100,000 in commissions for 10 consecutive years. These people spent 45 percent of their time prospecting — finding someone to talk to. They spent 20 percent of their time actually presenting — suggesting plans that they thought "made sense" to their contacts. They spent 20 percent of their time deepening their product knowledge and shaping what they offered to match what the product was looking to do. Finally, they devoted 15 percent of their time — far, far more than the average salesperson — to professional and personal development. This means learning new strategies, expanding intellectual horizons, and generally improving skills.

I've noticed that many of the successful senior executives I encounter have essentially the same list of priorities. They are constantly on the lookout for promising new business relationships; they aggressively promote plans that benefit themselves and their contacts; they find new ways to use their resources; and they take time to recharge their batteries and enrich themselves on a personal level so they can move past old limitations and outmoded belief systems.

Follow their example. Burst through those invisible glass walls and achieve at the very highest level.

MAKE IT HAPPEN PRINCIPLE 48

Commit to ongoing growth and development.

RULE 49 Think Big Enough to Outlast "Defeat"

Art Fry, a scientist at 3M Corporation and enterprising member of the local church choir, knew just what to do with a "failed" idea.

A colleague of Fry's had been working on developing a radical new formula for a revolutionary brand of adhesive. The objective had been to come up with a superior bonding agent, one that could revolutionize 3M's product line and capture the imagination — and the business — of a new generation of consumers. Unfortunately, the long process of experimentation had yielded a weak, vaguely gluey substance that delivered only the most tenuous attachment between objects. A single tug was enough to overcome the bond between whatever two items had (supposedly) been glued together.

The campaign to find the "hot" new adhesive had been a failure — a defeat. It hadn't produced the expected outcome.

Then came the Sunday morning when Art Fry found himself navigating the usual blizzard of paper bookmarks he used to keep track of the songs in his hymnal. "There has to be a better way to do this," he thought to himself. Then he remembered his colleague's failed experiment. Once back at work, he decided to take another look at the glue that wouldn't stick.

"I coated the adhesive on a paper sample," Fry recalls, "and I found that it was not only a good bookmark, but it was great for writing notes. It would stay in place as long as you wanted it to, and then you could remove it without damage." Fry had taken the result of a failure and used it to launch an idea that would become one of the biggest successes in the history of the 3M Corporation. When Art Fry coated one piece of paper with the new adhesive, and then applied that sheet of paper to another uncoated sheet, he created the world's first Post-It note!

Every "defeat" carries within it the seeds of victory.

I think Fry's story illustrates a principle that most of the world's accomplished entrepreneurs, salespeople, artists, social reformers, inventors, and innovators have understood and acted on habitually. It is this: *No experience is wasted, and no defeat final, as long as the human mind retains the power to think on a scale larger than past adversities.*

Think of Martin Luther King, who faced violence and opposition at every turn in his struggle to place civil rights on the national agenda. Think of Henry Ford, whose first auto business went bankrupt. Think of Mahatma Gandhi, a frail man in a prison cell taking on the whole of the British Empire. Think of Madame Curie, whose ideas about radium were ridiculed by the scientific establishment but who eventually became the first person, male or female, to win a second Nobel Prize.

How many "defeats" could these people have appealed to as justification for inaction, delay, or complacency? And yet each refused. Instead, each one changed the way a sizable number of people looked at the world. Time after time, history has demonstrated that the ability to think in a new and bold way very often attracts both resources and allies.

Certainly that's been my personal experience, and I think if you look back at the people in your own life who have most inspired you, you may discover much the same pattern. People who can assess a situation in a new way, who can effectively harness underutilized assets, are often the very ones who can move relationships forward, challenge old ways of thinking, and make good things happen for themselves and others.

It takes a little practice to become the kind of person who constantly examines the surroundings for new opportunities, new applications, and new ways of using existing resources. At our company, we have one word for this ability to reconfigure, reassess, and reawaken dormant possibility: *malleability.*

My dictionary defines malleability as "the quality of being moldable, flexible, pliable, or tractable; the state of being capable of adaptation or redirection when introduced to a new influence." I believe this definition applies both to the resources that make-it-happen people so constantly reevaluate and to the reevaluators themselves! What do I mean? I mean that the art of thinking big enough to outlast "defeat" demands not only that we look for ways to adapt the *tools* at our disposal, but also that we look for interesting ways to adapt our *own habits and preconceptions.*

So perhaps we start out looking for a great new adhesive, but if we look closely at the resources available to us, and open our own minds, we may realize that an entirely new product is waiting to be launched. Once we are willing to change *both* sides of the equation, we may just find that we can turn even a so-called defeat into a new opportunity for unparalleled achievement.

MAKE IT HAPPEN PRINCIPLE 49

Remember that no experience is wasted, and no defeat final, as long as the human mind retains the power to think on a scale larger than past adversities.

50 Failure Is a State of Mind... and Success Is a State of Action

Once I began a motivational program by asking, "How many certified failures are there in this room?" To my astonishment, about a dozen hands went up (out of a total attendance of about 100 people). I remember thinking to myself as I stared at those hands, "The act of nominating yourself as a failure — and nothing else — is what keeps you from taking action."

Failure exists, and we shouldn't persuade ourselves that it doesn't. But it exists solely as a state of mind. To the degree that we label ourselves failures, we are failures. On the other hand, I believe that people are aspirational animals. They are meant to commit themselves to things larger than themselves. That means, I submit, that we are all successes to the degree that we take action on what we aspire to. I truly believe that when we're in motion toward something worthwhile, we are successful.

Let me say it again. When we take some tangible action toward a constructive goal, we are, by definition, successes, because that's the time when we are actually moving toward our goals and focusing most clearly on our aspirations.

This, I believe, is the only really meaningful definition of a successful person: one who is moving toward an inspiring goal. How many wealthy but agonizingly unhappy people have you read about in your life? Successful people aren't born with better genes, or blessed with better looks, or in charge of more toys than unsuccessful people. Successful people are simply engaged in *doing* something about what they want to make happen in their lives.

That's my definition, at any rate. In support of it, I offer the following excerpt from the *Los Angeles Times* of February 7, 1985:

> A five-year study of 120 of the nation's top artists, athletes, and scholars has concluded that drive and determination, not great natural talent, led to their extraordinary success.
>
> "We expected to find tales of great natural gifts," said University of Chicago education professor Benjamin Bloom. . . . "We didn't find that at all. Their mothers often said it was their other child who had the greater gift. . . .
>
> "The most brilliant mathematicians often said they had trouble in school and were rarely the best in their classes."
>
> [T]he researchers heard accounts of an extraordinary drive and dedication through which, for example, a child would practice the piano several hours daily to attain his goal of becoming a concert pianist. A typical swimmer would tell of getting up at 5:30 every morning to swim two hours before school and then two hours after school to attain his or her goal of making the Olympic team.

May you never be without a passion or a plan for making it a reality — and may the tools I've shared with you in this book help you make the right things happen in your day, your career, and your life!

MAKE IT HAPPEN PRINCIPLE 50

The only point at which you can accurately say you have failed is the point at which you have stopped taking action on a meaningful goal.

Bibliography

Cox, Danny. *There Are No Limits*. Franklin Lakes, N.J.: Career Press, 1998.

King, Larry. *How to Talk to Anyone, Anytime, Anywhere: The Secrets of Good Conversation*. New York: Crown, 1994.

Lazar, Irving ("Swifty"), with Andrea Tapert. *Swifty: My Life and Good Times*. New York: Simon & Schuster, 1995.

National Business Employment Weekly (Premier Guides series). "Networking: Insiders' Strategies for Tapping the Hidden Market Where Most Jobs Are Found." New York: John Wiley & Sons, 1994.

Ray, Michael, and Rochelle Myers. *Creativity in Business*. Garden City, NY: Doubleday, 1986.

Robbins, Anthony. *Unlimited Power*. New York: Fireside, 1987.

Schiffman, Stephan. *Closing Techniques (That Really Work!)*, 2nd ed. Holbrook, Mass.: Adams Media, 1999.

_____. *Cold Calling Techniques (That Really Work!)*, 4th ed. Holbrook, Mass.: Adams Media, 1999.

_____. *High-Efficiency Selling*. New York: John Wiley & Sons, 1997.

Schwab, Charles. *Charles Schwab's Guide to Financial Independence: Simple Solutions for Busy People*. New York: Crown, 1998.

Toropov, Brandon. *301 Off-the-Wall Ways to Get a Job*. Franklin Lakes, New Jersey: Career Press, 1995.

Wallechinsky, David, and Irving Wallace. *The People's Almanac*. Garden City, NY: Doubleday, 1975.

Acknowledgments

This book would not be possible without the help, assistance, and input of Daniel Greenberg.

Make It Happen Before Lunch is a distillation of concepts I've developed over the past two decades as an entrepreneur. The ideas in the following pages are therefore a direct result of the love, advice, and support I've received from Anne and our daughters Jennifer and Daniele. I cannot thank them adequately here, but I can say that without them, none of D.E.I.'s success over the past thirty years would have been possible.

STEPHAN SCHIFFMAN

About the Author

Stephan Schiffman is a leader in motivational and sales training and a sought-after consultant and business strategist. He has been cited as "America's #1 Corporate Sales Trainer" and is acknowledged as the country's foremost expert in the area of prospecting skills. As founder and president of D.E.I. Management Group, he has overseen the training of nearly half a million professionals throughout the world in interactive seminars and workshops. He is the author of the bestselling business classic *Cold Calling Techniques (That Really Work!)*. His other books include *The 25 Habits of Highly Successful Salespeople, Make It Your Business,* and *The Consultant's Handbook.* Mr. Schiffman's systems have been implemented at companies like Aetna U.S. Healthcare, AT&T, Merill Lynch, MCI/WorldCom, Sprint, Exxon-Mobil, and Lexis-Nexis.